LETTERS FROM DOLLIE

Copyright © 2015 by Joaquin Bowman

**Marie McClary 1916 – 1996
(photo taken in 1944)**

**This book is dedicated to
Marie Sauerwald Collins McClary;
for her kindness and generosity and
forethought in preserving the memory
of Dollie McFarlane**

CONTENTS

THE POEMS

UNDERSTANDING DOLLIE

by Vibiana Bowman Cvetkovic

Reading *Letters from Dollie* is akin to over-hearing a fascinating, one-sided cell phone conversation. Thanks to the preservation efforts of Joaquin and Mary Ann Bowman, the *Dollie* reader is privileged to eavesdrop on the decades-long exchange (from the 1920s through to the 1940s) between Dorothy "Dollie" Clarke McFarlane and her dearest friend and confidant Margaret "Hazel" Hippler.

Dollie and Hazel were thought to have met in high school in Ardmore, Oklahoma. Their correspondence began when Hazel moved back East (to a Philadelphia suburb) in order to attend college. Dollie also moved away from home and got an office job in Arkansas City, Kansas. Missing her friend, Dollie wrote to

Hazel. Through these letters we (the readers) get a glimpse into a prairie woman's life in the first half of the twentieth century. What is compelling about this book, in addition to the rich detail and strong prose, is that we also must use our imagination in order to supply Hazel's counter-narrative.

Thus, we enter into our own conversation with Dollie. As a Childhood Studies and Popular Culture scholar, I am interested in American girlhood and *Letters from Dollie* enriches that field of study by providing a first person narrative illustrated with photographs. As such I hope that it finds a large audience, particularly with girls and young women, since it shines a light on what it meant to be female in a specific time and place in American history. So for a better understanding of Dollie I would like to give readers a little cultural perspective about this era.

Readers might wonder about the true nature of the relationship between Dollie and Hazel given the language of the letters. Dollie routinely uses terms that, according to today's conventions, would exclusively be used by romantic lovers. Gender Studies scholars have weighed in on what the correspondence of historical figures such as Abraham Lincoln and Emily Dickinson may, or may not, reveal about their sexuality.[1] One could argue that there is not enough evidence to draw a conclusion based on the letters alone. The writing style of the late-Victorian/Edwardian era, which was still influential when Dollie and Hazel were teens, tended to be more flowery and florid than the sparse prose of our post-Hemingway world. On the other hand, in the first part of the twentieth century physical relationships between young

---

[1] Interested readers may wish to consult Michael Ferguson's "Was Abraham Lincoln Gay?" in the *Journal Of Homosexuality* (2010) and Lewis Gannett's also in the *Journal Of Homosexuality* (2011).

women, while not socially accepted (indeed homosexual relationships were outlawed), were often viewed as a stage of sexual immaturity instead of a defining sexual identity. In short, female same-sex lovers were given a societal "pass" and their communities would turn a blind-eye, particularly if the young women eventually went on to marry and have families.[2] The reader can draw his or her own conclusion, but what the letters do substantiate is that Dollie cared very deeply for Hazel and deeply missed her friend.

As mentioned, Dollie and Hazel grew up in Oklahoma. In the early part of the twentieth century, many of the Western states were more progressive than those on the East Coast with regards to women's rights including women's suffrage. Wyoming, for example, the first state

---

[2] For more information about LGBQT history, particularly lesbians, see *Odd Girls and Twilight Lovers: A History of Lesbian Life in Twentieth-Century America* by Lillian Faderman (Columbian University Press, 2012).

to grant women the right to vote in 1869, also had the first woman governor, Nellie Tayloe Ross, who served from 1925 to 1927. Oklahoma traces its women's suffrage movement back to its Indian Territory days with initial lobbying efforts dating back to 1897.[3] This progressive stance has its roots in the ideal of the independent and courageous pioneer woman who settled the prairies and the American West. Historian Dee Brown notes that Western women have traditionally been given more cultural leeway in their performances of femininity than their Eastern counterparts.[4] Brown notes that the idealized Western woman was strong, tenacious, and self-reliant (p. 293). As women moved west in the mid-nineteenth century they realized that they were newly

---

[3] See the *Encyclopedia of Oklahoma History and Culture,* "Suffrage Amendment." Available http://digital.library.okstate.edu/encyclopedia/entries/S/SU002.htm l.
[4] See Dee Brown's *The Gentle Tamers Women of the Wild West* (University of Nebraska Press, 1957.)

unconstrained by East coast conventions in both mode of dress and behavior. They burst loose "from centuries of law and order" and their men admired them for it (p. 252). Because of the stress of lengthy travel to reach their new homes and the rigors of the work women by necessity were engaged in, a gender fluidity and "tomboy-ism" was tolerated, even encouraged. As Brown writes:

Rigid customs and nineteenth-century modesty in dress made overland travel difficult for the fairer sex. Recognizing this, one who had made the journey many times advised: "Side-saddles should be discarded—women should wear hunting frocks, loose pantaloons, men's hats and shoes, and ride the same as men." (p. 17)

The photograph of Dollie on the cover of this book is illustrative of this independent spirit. Dollie's body language exudes confidence: she is wearing beeches, her hair is cut in a stylish bob, and she gazes directly into the camera. She exemplifies Brown's description of the "Girl of the Golden West" as situated in the 1920s.

One of the most disturbing incidents described in the book is Dollie's brush with the Ku Klux Klan in Kansas ("Threats from the Klan.") This chapter recounts how when Dollie and group of friends, young men and women, go joy-riding out on the prairie and are confronted by a group of Klansmen. The Klansmen harass the group, letting them know that there could be repercussions for their unseemly behavior. Eventually let them go. In the 1920s the Klan was at its peak in the United States with a membership of over four million including 60,000 members in Kansas.[5] While the organization's most egregious acts of terrorism were against African Americans, Klansmen were anti-Semitic, anti-Catholic, and anti-immigrant. As is seen in Dollie's narrative, they also saw themselves as arbiters and enforcers of traditional American values, against what they deemed the corrupting forces of foreigners, non-Protestants, and an emerging notion of the independent woman.

I find it poignant to read the letters and follow the arc of Dollie's life from a strong-willed young woman to a settled-down wife and mother. In a last, long letter to Hazel in 1947 Dollie describes her life as a middle-aged woman in Oklahoma City, Oklahoma. The photos that she encloses show a slight woman, with downcast eyes and whose hair is pinned up

---

[5] See "Ku Klux Klan in Kansas." *Kansas Historical Society.* Available http://www.kshs.org/kansapedia/ku-klux-klan-in-kansas/15612.

in sensible braids. In this letter, which serves as our parting message from this amazing woman, the reader can still feel the wit and warmth of the girl that used to be. Dollie writes:

Looking at these pictures I must say I am doing my hair a different way, but it is the same old chassis. It was brought home to me how people change recently when the girl who preceded me in Joe's affections, and whom we have not seen in twenty years, wired us that she was coming through and came out at two in the morning and stayed until ten in the morning. When we knew her she was small and smart, and oh, soigneée. Now, well, it is apparent that the years have gone over. So I cannot feel that I am unaltered. In fact, I know damn well I'm not.

This is a really very long letter, and it is late and I must rise early, so shall cease here. I do hope that neither sickness nor misunderstanding interferes with our meeting the next time. It is possible I may go north again to see my mother soon and, if I do, I will certainly try to see you.

Love, Dollie

Vibiana Bowman Cvetkovic is a Reference Librarian at Rutgers University in New Jersey and American Popular Culture scholar. She is a doctoral candidate in the Childhood Studies Department at Rutgers Camden and her area of research and writing is the depiction of childhood in popular culture. Ms. Cvetkovic is the author of several peer-reviewed journal articles, encyclopedia journal articles and has edited several books. Her most recent publications include: "Feminine Mystique: *Superman's Girl Friend Lois Lane in the 'Silver Age' of Comics*" (in *Examining Lois Lane* edited by Nadine Farghaly, Scarecrow Press, 2013); *Portrayals of Children in Popular Culture: Fleeting Images* (Lexington Books, 2014); and *Reinventing Reference: How Libraries Deliver Value in the Age of Google* (American Library Association, 2015).

WHAT'S IT ALL ABOUT?

Letters from Dollie is a very personal story about a talented writer and a free-thinking feminist who immigrated with her family from Ireland when she was 11 and matured into an adult in rural Oklahoma in the first half of the twentieth century.

Dollie describes her life as young woman, office worker, wife and mother, much of it through her correspondence with her girlhood friend, Hazel Hippler, later McClary, of Pennsylvania.

I knew very little about Dollie's early life, except what was told to me by my mother-in-law, Marie McClary, in the form of oral history passed from Hazel to her husband Harold "Mac" to Marie, then to me. Later, in her letters, Dollie talks openly about her life and feelings.

Dollie's eyewitness accounts bring a unique and personal perspective to American history of the 1920s, ´30s and ´40s and chronicle phenomena such as the influence of the Ku Klux Klan, the Oklahoma oil boom, and the poverty of farmers in the Dust Bowl.

I tried through both the Genealogy Library of Ardmore, Oklahoma and Arkansas City Historical Society in Arkansas City, Kansas to find information about Dollie and her family, but struck out. Through Ancestry.com I was able to come up with a few details about Dollie and her husband, Joe, but not much on the two children she references in her letters. I feel, however, that Dollie's story is well worth preserving, even if parts of her life are simply based on oral history and historical reconstructions.

Unfortunately, there is no record of any letters Hazel sent to Dollie. We know the two women were much different and the contrast provides the canvass for their relationship. Through all appearances, Dollie tried to fashion her friend into a more daring and risk taking individual. While her efforts generally failed, her love of Hazel never wavered.

The wit and wisdom contained in *Letters from Dollie* provide insights into her relationship with Hazel and an opportunity to share the emotions and experiences of this bright and fascinating woman.

Through writing this book I developed a kinship with this avant-garde woman and thought of her often since I started this project almost 20 years ago.

I would love to have more information about Dorothy Maude Clarke McFarlane. She includes some details about her daughter Ann in her letters along with a photo of this lovely girl. I believe Dollie also had a son, Joe Patrick. If readers have information on Dollie, her family and copies of her writings, I'd love to have them and possibly use updates for a revised edition of this book. I can be reached at: trego2@comcast.net

Finally, I would like to thank my wife, Mary Ann, my sister, Vibiana Cvetkovic, and good friend Michael Schluth for their help with this book.

Joaquin Bowman

DISCOVERY

Willow Grove, Pennsylvania
March 1996

It was a job that had to be done. Like they say, "somebody has to do it."

Trash cans, three of them, were faithfully lined up waiting patiently to be filled, dumped, to be filled again, dumped, and so on.

These were the collections, papers, odds and ends of a person's life and it was my unpleasant duty to sift through the boxes and decide what had value and what should be tossed away.

"Do we really need to save your grandfather's telephone bills from 1973?" I called to my wife Mary Ann who was stretched out on the couch reading a gothic romance novel.

"No," she said weakly.

This job, the process of going through her recently deceased mother's "effects" was simply too painful for my wife, the only child of the union of Frank and Marie.

Marie, who had died of bone cancer a few weeks before was the best mother-in-law, I believe, a man could have. She was kind and generous and loved my two children as if they were her own "blood" grandchildren. When Mary Ann and I married, we each had two children, all about the same age, a kind of a "Brady Bunch" I called them, trying to make it sound okay to have a family with different parents. Actually it was okay, the kids got along and we managed to keep our family and marriage intact.

So there we were, Mary Ann on the couch and me going through the boxes of her mother's things.

"Did your mother have a Nash Rambler? I got some paper here from 1963. It says she bought it new. Stick shift. No radio."

"Yes, toss it," she said.

That purchase was made after Mary Ann's father, an Italian housing contractor, lost his business and decided it was best for all concerned if he simply left the state. It wasn't easy for the two women he left behind, one 15, the other a 44-year-old housewife who hadn't held a job for a quarter century and was scared of losing everything. By hard work and sheer determination she managed to land on her feet and get the last laugh on old Frank who died penniless.

Marie lost the suburban brick house, but then got a job, in fact two jobs, one answering phones on a midnight shift, the other clerking in a candy store. She rented an apartment for the two of them, put Mary Ann through school, giving her a decent start in life.

Eventually, after Mary Ann got married, Marie took care of her elderly, proud, Austrian father until he died, then got the title to his suburban house, a kind of practical pig house, he built in the 1940s. She raised her daughter and now had a nice, comfortable home in her name. No one could touch it. It was hers.

Shortly afterward she met a widower, Harold "Mac" Benjamin McClary, then 81, and quickly got married since Mac said he didn't have time to waste. Marie nursed him when he got ill and inherited his New Jersey property when he died at 88. She now had two houses, free and clear.

If this was Monopoly she would have been well on her way to winning the game.

Marie died six years later, everything went to Mary Ann, an only child, and there I was sorting out the "boxes." The big stuff was gone. We had the garage sales, sold the furniture, let the kids take what they wanted and packed everything else, from two houses, into these dozen or so boxes now sitting in the dining room waiting for me, "Mr. Organization," to decide what's valuable.

"Why did they save oil bills?" I called to Mary Ann. "I have oil bills from 1940. I have your grandfather's oil bills, you mother's oil bills, and Mac's. Did they think they would be able to redeem them for a toaster? Collect $10,000 in ancient oil bills and get a toaster?"

"Toss 'em," she mumbled.

That was good enough for me. Out they went. Thud! In the trash.

The three trash containers were nearly ready for another dumping.

"Mary Ann, what's in this orange carton tied with a string? It's in the bottom of the oil bill box," I continued hoping she would know and tell me to dump it.

"Letters," she replied. "I need to look at them."

With that, she rose from the couch and came walking into the dining room, carelessly stepping on papers I was sorting on the floor. It was painful for her to look at these relics, going back to her childhood, reminding her of the house her grandfather built, her father's failing business and the passing of her mother.

"These are the letters my mother talked about, enjoyed, and asked me to read," she said. "Maybe you would like to look at them," she offered, hoping I would, and make the final decision regarding their fate.

"Please," I begged, "I can't look at everything. If you don't care to see them, out they go," I threatened.

She walked slowly back to the couch, picked up her book and lost herself in it once again. She knew I would save the letters out of respect for her mother and because of my own curiosity.

. . . *five months later*

Doylestown, Pennsylvania

A few months after the "dirty deed" was done and the discarded belongings had been taken by "Mr. Trashman," I took an early retirement from my job at the transportation company and began, after 31 years of nine-to-five, to do very little.

One of the challenges on my "Things To Do" list was to clean my attic "collection room." It was my part of the house, cluttered with an outdated computer that was left over after we bought our new Gateway, an assortment of autographic Kodak cameras, and early Disneyana (Mickey Mouse stuff, some going back to 1931). Tucked under the desk were the letters my mother-in-law had packed away; ones my guilt and curiosity prevented me from trashing months before.

"I should have thrown them out when I had the chance," I thought to myself, "Mary Ann would have never known the difference."

I was glad I didn't.

Sitting upstairs that afternoon as I scanned the first letter from the neatly tied bundle, I felt my mother-in-law was sitting with me. Directing me. On the envelope of the top letter, scrawled in her handwriting were the words "Dollie married." It was simple but somehow moved me to open the yellowed envelope addressed to Mrs. H. B. McClary of McDaniels Avenue in Dayton, Ohio.

It began: **My Dearest Friend: Perhaps I was abrupt, but so was my decision to marry.**

The date was May 31, 1926.

The letter went on to explain that she had only known Joe McFarlane for six weeks before they married "quietly and circumspectly." She talked about how happy they were together, how kind he was and good looking.

" . . . and I had not known that life could be so very dear. I love. I am loved. We're young. The gods are kind. Too kind and sometimes I fear they may become jealous of my happiness."

The letter concluded: Here's my love, Dollie.

Attached, fastened by a straight pin, was a small newspaper clipping about their "living room" wedding in the home of a friend. "Mrs. McFarlane, a young girl, possesses much charm and personality," it stated.

I was moved and realized my mother-in-law's wisdom in saving these letters. I read on.

At times, tears filled my eyes. For me, Dollie was real; as I'm sure she was for my mother-in-law. As I picked up letters one by one, I looked for my mother-in-law's brief summary penciled carefully, thoughtfully on each envelope and read on.

I came to know a woman ahead of her time. Not the mainstream, everyday girl, but a whole person who longed to taste, smell and touch the essence of her experiences and tell about it in letters to her conservative friend, her pal. She did not hide her pain and her joy, as so many others who were trained to suppress their emotions. Most importantly, Dollie was gifted in her ability to put her feelings into words.

I also came to know and appreciate another fine woman, Marie McClary, my mother-in-law. The simple fact that she preserved and cherished this rich history of Dollie McFarlane is evidence that she too experienced the same feelings and emotions I felt when reading these letters.

I knew the letters were important, too important to be kept in a box. So now, I am sharing them with you.

THE BEGINNING

Dorothy "Dollie" Maude Clarke of
Ireland entered the world on February 7, 1905.
Her mother Florence was 22 at the time.

Dollie was the oldest of three girls. Her
sister, Blanche, was born in 1906 and Florence,
(named after her mother) in 1909.

This information on Dollie's family came
from the ship's manifest when they immigrated
to the United States from Liverpool, England in
1916 aboard the SS Tuscania and arrived in

 New York on
February 24.
There was no
information
on Dollie's
father on the passenger list nor does Dollie refer

to him in any of her letters. He may have been deceased when they left Ireland.

Incidentally, the SS Tuscania, which carried up to 2500 passengers, launched in 1914, was sunk by a German U-boat in 1918.

Dollie speaks fondly of Ireland in a letter she sent to Hazel in 1947 when she was 42 years old. This is what she said:

"The Arbuckles (The Arbuckle Mountains are an ancient mountain range in

 south-central Oklahoma) really are almost my hills of home, for I almost

forgotten the little, soft green hills of Ireland (but never quite) and my courting was done in and around the Arbuckles in one lovely April and May."

Why the family came to the United States and settled in Oklahoma is anyone's guess. Perhaps they had family here, but that is hard to ascertain from Dollie's letters.

What's certain is that Dollie was very smart and quick-witted. She was not a shrinking violet and would not back away from a fight or even an ugly confrontation. Later she takes on the huge responsibility of running a farm, slaughtering livestock and raising children almost singlehandedly while her husband Joe was away earning a living in the oil industry.

Life was not easy for Dollie, though she never complains. In fact, in 1941, she writes:

"But I can't remember when I had so much fun. I get up at five thirty, and work hard until six in the evening, then crochet or read after the rest of the family has gone off to bed."

By 1947 Dollie was running a 150-acre farm, planting crops, handling the farm animals and raising children. She was still writing and running a "cottage industry" of making dolls in period costumes, sort of a forerunner of *American Girl* dolls.

She was an amazing and talented woman. This is her life starting with Hazel's recollections of her dear friend.

THE EARLY YEARS

Apart from the letters, Dollie told her friend Hazel stories about her early life in Ireland.

"I didn't take nonsense from anyone," she proudly announced. As a six-year-old, when an older cousin challenged her in arm wrestling, she lost and quickly punched him in the nose for laughing at her.

"Grow up," she shouted over her shoulder as he chased her back to the safety of her home. She easily outran the boy.

Dollie earned a reputation as a bit of a tomboy. She didn't care one iota and kind of liked the idea of being a rebel in their conservative farming community.

Hazel said that Dollie kept the family well stocked with various vegetables, fruits and eggs which she proudly stole from the neighbors.

Her mother never told her husband where the food came from; she was glad to get it but felt obliged to scold Dollie for stealing. Secretly, however, she admired her ingenuity for getting away with it. No one ever suspected this tiny, although smart-mouthed, creature with pilfering their goods.

One day, Dollie went out on a "hunt" and found a supply of salted meats drying in Mr. Butler's smoke shack. The pork looked especially appetizing and she was tempted to take only enough for a family meal. As she was thinking it over, Mr. Butler's dog Dash wandered in and spotted Dollie.

Although Dash was not aggressive, Dollie suspected that if she went toward the tasty meat hanging from hooks attached to the crossbeams, there could be trouble. Wisely, Dollie patted Dash on the head, gave him a snack from her pocket, and got a sloppy lick on her arm, and left.

As a student Dollie excelled.

She was quick to learn, having picked up reading and math from her father who loved to

read to Dollie while Mother did her sewing on a rocker near the fireplace. The adventure stories written by Mark Twain and Robert Louis Stevenson were among their favorites. Dollie imagined herself as a character in Tom Sawyer, having all sorts of fun and dangerous escapades. Dollie viewed her childhood as one, never ending adventure. Her imagination was in high gear day and night. Stealing chicken eggs just added to the fun.

Family members were leaving Ireland for the United States to make their fortune in the big cities like New York and Chicago. When they found work in the slaughter houses and factories they would often send a few dollars to the relatives back home.

In addition to high rates of unemployment, disease and overall lack of food, there was political unrest in much of the country. In December of 1915, the Irish Republican Brotherhood Military Council decided to stage an uprising the following Easter.

The Clarkes were struggling to survive in Ireland and, anticipating greater opportunities of finding employment in the United States, the family moved to Ardmore, Oklahoma.

Details about why they chose that portion of the United States are unknown.

THE ENCOUNTER

In 1920, as a 15-year-old, Dollie was maturing into a slightly rough-around-the-edges, but attractive young woman. Her slightly olive complexion and shapely curves caught the attention of the boys in her high school but they found her independent attitude intimidating.

Most girls her age were grooming themselves to get married after graduation and raise a house full of kids, much like their mothers. But Dollie had other plans. Her desire was to make something of herself and get out of "Hicksville" as soon as humanly possible.

 **Strangely enough Dollie's best friend in town was a fellow classmate named Margaret Hazel Hippler, known to friends simply as Hazel .**

Hazel was the polar opposite of Dollie. She delighted in sewing, making her own clothes, mostly dresses and other girly things. Dollie wore pants, knickers and the like, often buying her wardrobe in the boy's section of the Clemmer Department store in town.

Sure, kids made fun of her, but she was likely to tell them to, "Stuff it." She didn't care. She did what worked for her and she was satisfied.

But Dollie formed a kinship with Hazel that was hard to explain. Although Hazel lacked Dollie's adventurous spirit, she was a terrific listener and Dollie kept her spellbound retelling from memory the stories her Dad had read to her.

They could talk for hours sitting on porch steps sipping cold drinks on hot afternoons.

Dollie told Hazel about one of the boys in her class, Scott Butler, who would occasionally look over at her in biology and sometimes they would greet in the halls as they traveled from class to class.

One afternoon Scott followed her from school and offered to carry her books on their way home. Of course, she was flattered. No boy ever offered to walk with her and attempt a "conversation." Dollie was enjoying having the company of the handsome young man and felt flattered he wanted to be with her.

As they neared Dollie's home Scott moved closer to return Dollie's books and in a flash kissed her directly on the lips. At that moment a group of boys, hiding behind a tall shrub, jumped out and started cheering.

"Scott, you're the man!" one boy yelled.

Dollie was shocked. Apparently Scott's feigned interest was all a ruse; nothing more than a bet with his friends he could steal a kiss with the tomboy before they reached her front steps.

Scott won and Dollie was horrified and angry she was made the fool.

Then Dollie sat down on the steps, and for the first time in her memory, she cried.

She never had a real boyfriend and, at 15, wasn't sure where her heart was leading her. She saw what happened with other local girls and had no intention of getting herself "knocked up."

Of course, the next day at school, news of the incident spread like wildfire. Dollie was the "chump" and she told herself it would never happen again.

Hazel told her, "Like everything else, this will pass." Dollie was determined, however, to get that Scott Butler and his pack of "turds" and make them pay for what they did.

Hazel advised her to let it go. "What goes around, comes around," she told her friend. But Dollie was determined that, if the opportunity ever presented itself, she'd like to make it "come around" a little sooner.

Hazel was right, of course, the matter was soon forgotten.

Despite the prank, Dollie found Scott Butler attractive, maybe because he was daring. A bit like her.

"Let me tell you, sweetie, that boy can park his shoes under my bed whenever he wants. If he wants to steal a kiss from me, I'd tell him to come on over," Hazel told her.

As strange as it seems, within a few days, Scott apologized to Dollie for the prank and asked her to forgive him. In the back of her mind Dollie thought that maybe Scott might be a bit frightened that she would get him back, but he seemed sincere so they agreed to bury the hatchet. Scott asked her out for an evening at the local cinema.

The evening went well. Scott was a good talker, much like Dollie's father and also enjoyed having "adventures." But when he went to kiss her on their walk home she hesitated and he got the message. She wasn't going to be made the fool ever again.

"Don't you like me?" Scott asked.

"It's not that, Scott. Sure I like you. In fact, I like you a lot," Dollie responded. "But for now let's just keep it that way."

But Scott was not dissuaded and tried again before they reached Dollie's front yard. Before she knew it Dollie McFadden got her first real kiss from a boy. And this time no one jumped up from behind the bushes.

Scott was strong and held her tightly. Dollie quietly let Scott fold her in his muscular embrace and felt his warmth surround her.

She watched her parents embrace and now knew firsthand what it was like to be held in such a way.

Now, as the perfect gentleman, Scott walked her to the door, kissed her on top of her head and she went in.

The next day she told Hazel all about it.

"Good for you," Hazel said. Then when Dollie told her friend about Scott's interest, Hazel gave her the best advice she would ever receive, "Go with your heart, sweetie. Just go with your heart."

Hazel's words would prove to be a guiding force throughout her life.

FOLLOW YOUR HEART

Dollie remembered those words spoken by Hazel and worked hard in school to take the business courses that would eventually prepare her for office work and a job far away from Ardmore, Oklahoma.

She often thought about her cousins, making a success of their lives 900 miles north in the Chicago slaughter houses and, while most girls her age were content to marry a local boy and stay close to their mothers, she was not.

Dollie found that she had a talent for writing and contributed a few articles to the high school paper, *The Torch*. Her first contribution, *Lonely Skies*, attracted some attention from the local newspaper and won a $5 prize awarded by the Grange.

Another, which she called *Chimney on the Prairie,* appeared in the local paper. This is what she wrote:

Once there must have been a house here –
No one would build a chimney of stone
And let it stand, year after year,
Like an old tower, crumbling, alone.
Birds nest in it. I should say
They are martens, all purple black,
Martens like houses, they must stay
Wanting their walls and people back.
One generation after another
Hatching out, flying and mating,
Nesting in the vines that smother
The stone, the martens waiting
For good log walls and the woman who
Talked to them and scattered crumbs
As sometimes lonely women do.
One thing I know, she had green thumbs,

Coaxed from cutting the roses growing
Beside the chimney standing there.
Perhaps she is dust whose flowers,
blowing,
Sweeten this place and make it fair.
I think these better than marble shaft or
Headstone engraved with decorous
words,
Her roses, shaken by the wind's laughter
And the brave flight of her small birds.

Dollie was on her way. With some
encouragement from Hazel, she began making

weekly contributions to
her weekly local paper.
She did a nicely written
column, and readers
loved it. Her column
was called HemLines.

Her short articles
gave advice to mothers
on homemaking and

caring for small children. She drew on her own knowledge by watching her mother and younger sisters and found it easy to pen a couple paragraphs, which sometimes brought responses from readers. Hazel was a pretty good seamstress and would provide suggestions on making clothes and keeping a budget. The girls made a great team.

Mr. Samson, the kindly editor, even offered Dollie a job if, "She would stick to her writing and finish high school."

Dollie wasn't interested, but was flattered by Mr. Samson's offer, nonetheless. Even if she never made it to Chicago she was only about 90 miles from Oklahoma City and, if worse came to worse, she would make a move there. Hazel agreed and the young women talked about perhaps moving there together.

ON HER OWN

Sadly, after high school graduation, Dollie and Hazel parted ways.

Hazel had family back East, near Philadelphia, and decided to enroll in one of the schools and possibly earn a college degree and become a teacher.

Dollie, on the other hand, took a job at the Red Grange Mill as an office worker. She continued her columns at *The Daily Ardmoreite* and took courses at night to learn business.

Then in 1923 when Dollie was 18 she saw an ad for an junior office manager at the Ark Petroleum Company in Arkansas City, Kansas, about 225 miles north of her home in Ardmore.

 **This was a significant leap for Dollie but she saw Hazel make a major change in her life and knew it was now or never.**

Off went Dollie's application letter and within a few days she was asked to take the train north for the interview. Dollie could write and take shorthand and they were obviously impressed with the energetic young woman.

Her life in Arkansas City was the direct opposite of what she experienced in her first 18 years. There was a feeling of excitement at Ark Petroleum and the Irish lass soon became the

focus of the bright young men who worked with her in the office.

Soon, lonely for her friend, she began sending long letters to Hazel describing the daily events in her life. The letters span a 24 year period, with long gaps – some for several years. We'll never know why, but we are fortunate to have this record of Dollie's life, though incomplete.

GHASTLY, GHOSTLY FIGURES

June 5, 1923
Arkansas City, Kansas

Sweets:

Went to the Roxana office today for another couple of days. Strange, the attraction I seem to hold for lovely boys - I can find no explanation for it, can you? But to revert - a miserable youth from St. Louis asked me to lunch with him, and we had a glorious time, both talking at once, each oblivious to the other's remarks, about the respective beauties of Philly (Philadelphia) and St. Louis.

Then, when I came home, I found no mail and was very lonely and discouraged, but

Mother (here for a visit) dragged me off for a ride, babbling about some business venture. I took the little kitten with me and we sat in the back seat and gloried in the evening. Sunset - a molten lake of gold in the West, the eastern clouds flushed a delicate rose, against a pastel blue sky. Below, trees a feathery mass of contrasting greens and brown, and the scent of purified fields of alfalfa, sweet in my nostrils.

So to Winfield, and then the road back. We had not gone far, when, against a patchy sky, I saw a gleam of red. As we drew nearer, I saw distinctly the outlines of a fiery cross. First I shook myself - then pinched myself gingerly, blinked my eyes, wagged my head and looked again. Still there burned the cross against the night. "What," thought I, "is the matter with me? There couldn't possibly be a church in the middle of the field. I haven't been drinking. Am I dying? Yes, that must be it - of course,

 I'm bound for hell, but before I slide down to eternal damnation, the Lord is vouchsafing me the glimpse of the cross. But it really isn't a well-staged death scene, without an angel. Whereupon three ghostly, ghastly white figures appeared as though from the air.

"Good Lord," think I, "You're doing me proud! Three angels! At least I'm going out in a blaze of glory, though I lived in ignominious obscurity." Just then, one of the angels thrust back his snowy robes and put his hands in his trousers pockets, and puffed on a cigarette. "Celestial fire!" I exclaimed to myself. "Ku Klux Klan!"

And so it was. They were having an initiation, and they are very strong down here.

Philandering husbands are whipped and returned forcibly to the arms of their loving wives. Dissolute youth does not go unpunished. Neckers in parked cars out in the country are surrounded, seized and whipped. Drunks also. In fact, law and order are enforced by mob rule, you might say.

Lord, can you imagine the number of Klansmen it would take to whip the neckers in Fairmount Park (in Philadelphia)?

Awfully tired now, so shall pop into bed to dream of white-robed Klansmen breathing flame and smoke, chasing me across country in Fords (an unromantic machine, which seems to have replaced the horse as their means of transportation).

Tomorrow or Wednesday. And back again. Still no letter from you.

I worked in the office today, as they needed an extra girl. So many men are employed in the field, and today a very pitiful old chap came in. Painfully clean, torn and darned shirt, dusty trousers and cracked, muddy boots; battered, old felt hat and a small bundle in his hand. Tiredly, he went up to the employment man; an ingratiating half fearful smile splitting his thin, red, weather-beaten face into a thousand wrinkles.

"Pardon me, suh. Is my son (mentioning the name) employed here?" A curt denial

"You're sure, suh? I've walked nearly all over the United States lookin' for him. I wouldn't want to miss him now - I'm so near the end of my journey. He was such a good boy, suh, but fell upon evil ways -drinkin' and gamblin'. It broke his mother's heart when he left. Ran away, suh, and she died in my arms. He meant no wrong, suh, he was only twenty-one and such a good boy, and I haven't seen him now for five years but wherever there are engineers and oil fields, I go and ask. I've a deed for the little place in Carolina, suh, and it's his, if he'll only come back to me. He was so like his mother, suh, and I'm very lonely. He isn't here, you say?"

Very abrupt and discourteous negation.

"Thank you, suh, and good day." And putting the old, worn hat on his sparse, white hair, he turned to start wearily on his fruitless search, invested with a splendid dignity of age and right. Oh, Hazel, I wanted so to take him home, and find that careless, thoughtless, "very good boy, who was so much like his mother," for him. I went out into the ladies room and wept a little, and prayed a little that in the last, before he came "to the end of his journey," he'd find his lad.

I have decided to call my little black kitten Skunkie, for reasons best not inquired into.

Tonight I went to see a poor boy who is very ill with tonsillitis - somehow everything seems so pathetic of late.

There isn't much more to say, save the timeworn refrain - I love you. I will come back to you, for oh, I miss you so, dearest of all. Wait for me - we've made each other do that for hours now and I asking you to do it for months - and I know you will.

I am, dearest, you know wholly and implicitly yours.

Dollie

OVERWHELMING HEAT

June 11, 1923
Arkansas City, Kansas

My Dearest Hazel:

Drove home at lunch today and to be the recipient of a note from you nearly floored me.

Oh sweets, sweets your illness isn't dangerous (unknown) is it? You only need rest and care, don't you? And it would be best if you go to Atlantic City; enjoy the sea breezes, sunsets, bronzed life guards and enough time, perhaps, to write me more often.

Dearest, I am praying that you are well soon, and be the merry old girl I knew, and loved. So healthy, so strong. No headaches and bad nerves. Just young and healthy, my own dearest.

And, I will write to you every day, and think of you and love you all the while, so that if there is such a thing as faith-healing, you should soon find yourself free of pain.

I'm very hot, dearest. We have it so awfully, accursedly warm and the perspiration forms in beads about my upper lip and my eyes. There isn't a way to escape the heat – I almost envy your illness for you will find certain solace in the moods of the whimsical ocean that I am denied here in this godforsaken place. But you must get well so that I may find you r'aring to go when I come back east. A husky Hazel!

My mind keeps coming back to the heat.

All afternoon I wiped the perspiration from various portions of my anatomy and have watched the heat simmer in waves out of the ground. Watched sombreroed tanned men drive horses, white with lather, across sandy hollows. To turn and typewrite madly, wipe away more sweat, turn and watch tractors crawl through the blazing sunshine. There a line of trees, greener than grass, against the blue, burning skyline. A mule team passes; the mules back their heads to bray with disgust at the intensity of the heat. It's frightful – I've never experienced anything like it – I'm radiating heat like one of those beastly old-fashioned German porcelain stoves.

Tonight, perhaps, I'll go for a ride with Herbert in his car. Down the main drag – to see cheap flappers, cake eaters and men in black velvet flaring trousers with inserts of red and rows of bells. There's sure to be Osage Indians – swarthy, handsome and dressed richly and in good taste, save for a rather conspicuous but beautiful wide Panama hats. The girls dress in the latest styles, regardless of their figures or coloring.

Oh Hazel, I'm so damn hot – but I got to get back to work, or it will be much longer before I can come back to you, and that must be soon.

Dearest, remember you must get well, and belong wholly to me.

Your Dollie

RETURN OF ULYSSES

Dollie's talent as a gifted writer was demonstrated in the rich language she uses in her letters to Hazel.

Nothing seems forced.

Her descriptions are incredible.

Sombreroed tanned men drive horses, white with lather, across sandy hollows.

Dollie was gifted.

Mixed with the letters I found a few poems she had published. Unfortunately I am unable to find when or where.

This is one example:

RETURN OF ULYSSES

He came back. Everything was just the same.

There was the long, sad whistle of
the train,
The spire of the church against the
sky of flame.
There were the children,
rollerskating on Main
Because it was the one paved street
in town.
There were the boys shouting, bring
home cows
With heavy pointed teats, cows
bridled and brown,
Dignified, short stepping, with
impressive brows.
It was as he remembered, it was all
there,
The same houses and trees, there
was no change,
Save for an alien coldness in the air,
Save for the knowledge only he was
strange.

THE ENTIRE COUNTY IS UNDERWATER

June 12, 1923
Arkansas City, Kansas

Tuesday-

Last night about twelve thirty as I put the finishing touches on my letter to you, a car drove up and one of the girls, escorted by Red Miller, whose face was pale green beneath his flowing shock of hair, came in and asked for shelter. So I gave her my bed and slept (very little) on my army cot.

They say the water is slowly going down but I won't be able to receive or send mail for forty eight hours. At four o'clock this morning the engineers in the warehouse were taken off - every man was up all night, Bob sending trucks

71

and teams and boats to the relief all the time. Mother and I made coffee and piles of ham sandwiches and took them up late at night, and to see those oil-soaked, eager, exhausted chaps dig into them was pitiful. The company comedian, Mr. Thomen, who was stranded on a knoll until four, was in real danger, and had for company a cow, a pig, a mule and a snake that had been driven there for safety. The snake, which was poisonous, he killed with a stone, and just a little later, the mule, stricken with melancholia, plunged in the water, a suicide. Thomen is one of the best chaps I've ever met, and to hear him tell of his really perilous adventure is rib-splitting. Red Miller is knocked out, Allen is a total loss, everyone having played heroic roles, is now on the verge of complete collapse. Really, it's harder on the women than the men, for they can only sit at home and think, while the men can work.

Just went uptown and lunched with Red Miller and Allen. Funny incidents begin to be told - of the man wading shoulder-deep through the torrent with an open umbrella to protect his head from the rain; of the rival black kids on two rafts, one of whom spent the night pulling chickens onto the raft, the other who got every

 snake in Kansas; of Red tired out, wading back, who sighted a five gallon demijohn floating downstream and emitted a wild Texas "Yahoo" and sprang in like a spring chicken to secure the evidence; of the sheriff, who walked into the office, half shot, and plunked down a quart of whiskey saying, "Thar ye are boys, it'll cheer you up. It's good, I've been drinkin' it all night myself."

Of course, the water and electric lights have been cut off all over town, and taps and toilets refuse to function. "Little gray homes in the West" or outhouses are in great demand. We're fairly lucky as we have a pump and cistern water in the shed, and my famous right arm feels worn off to the shoulder as I've been pumping water to give Red a bath. He has just gone in and beseeches me to scrub his back. Pardon, I hear his most unmelodious voice. He said when I arrived "I really don't want you to scrub my back, but I'd like a bucket of cold water. This bath so hot my body will be the color of my hair, if I risk it."

Well, finished dinner, and after that received Red and Mr. Allen in our sitting room - blaa-blaa! Red accommodatingly whipped me with my swagger stick - I further infuriated Mr. Allen so that he finally, after he had racked his brain for sarcastic retorts - he fled, which was not at all what I desired. Damn the man, he's awfully good looking, conceited and spoiled by the adulation of impressionable hick girls, so it's up to me to take some of the swell-headedness out of him.

Red and I sat on the porch until one o'clock, discussing the flood, the town as it is, under martial law, love, pals, and a mutual vow to remain single and have our grandchildren do likewise.

At last I heard the whistle of a train and as they must be able to come through, I'll post this narrative tomorrow. Now, I going to bed, tired out with the events of the last two days, and comforted by the thought that I soon may receive mail. Good night, beloved

Wednesday, June 13 -

Here I am again. There nothing much to say - or do. The water is down about three feet, but everyone feels a little wary as they go about with crossed fingers.

It was pretty dangerous while it lasted, but with the aid of Bryce and Red I got the first real kick out of anything I've had since I came west.

It was fun, spiced with danger and my only regret is that they wouldn't allow me to work with the boys. It's hell being a girl and having to stick around.

I just received a five-pound box of chocolates from Bryce and a box of lovely writing paper from Red with the inscription -

"To write to my rival in the East. May every page cause him heart break." Nice?

Must post this now - and see if everything is OK in the house.

Will write you tomorrow. Be sure (as you are) that I am, Your Dollie

Sunday Afternoon, June 17

The entire county is under water and trains cannot come in or leave. Pretty sad state of affairs.

Last night Mr. Greenshields, Mr. Court (the Englishman), Mother, Bob and Mr. Blizzard and I started off to Winfield for some of that celebrated limeade. It was not until we reached the Walnut River Bridge that we found the way barred and the road a swiftly moving stream of water. Back we came to town, took Mr. Blizzard and Bill home and then started to take Mr. Greenshields back. As we dropped him at his door his roommate walked up, a Mr. Allen, and the most fascinating man I've seen

since I left town! He's very blonde, blue eyed, about six foot and I swear he looks good enough to eat, so that my mouth waters every time I see him. But the damn fool treats me like a ten year old and I could slay him! Curses! He won't pay any attention to me. So after being as beastly to him as I could, we came home.

This morning early, all the Roxana engineers were called out because the construction offices were threatened by the flood. Forgetting all my grievances with Bob, I donned a pair of his riding breeches (which reminds me, why in the name of God don't you send my knickers?) and a khaki shirt, climbed in the car and we drove as near the site as possible. Ten yards further the road was impassable, so we commandeered a mule team and drove over or through, I should say. Arriving safely, we hopped off into the mud, and the first person I bumped into was the handsome Mr. Allen. I, with forethought, had loaded myself to the gunwales with cigarettes, so he and the others greeted me with great joy. Then they planted me in a cherry tree, telling me to eat cherries and be a good little girl while they worked. After a time they came back and we started down the road, the water rippling down the fields on either side.

Suddenly I sighted some little chickens marooned on a tiny patch of land, and clamored loud and long to be taken to rescue. So, Mr. Allen and Bryce Greenshields, looking like Puss in Boots with their rubber high boots, made a chair of their hands and carried me over, plumped me down on the sand and left me. Whereupon, I collected the chickens, philosophically lighted one remaining cigarette, and sat down in the mud, which squished discouragedly about the seat of my pants.

Presently, I heard an "Ahoy!" and saw Bryce Greenshields punting an empty (save for himself) water tank with a fishing pole towards my island which was gradually lessening in size. In I climbed and we aimlessly drifted over towards the top of some remarkably fine cherry trees, where we lingered.

On consuming the half ripe fruit we were smitten with the pangs of collywobbles, so we made a gallant fight against the current, beached our ungainly craft upon a sand bank, and Bryce carried me across the other stream before the road "a la fireman," by one ankle and wrist over his manly shoulder. Caught the mule team back, loaded into its coffin shaped wagon a discouraged hungry crowd of engineers - and me. Of course, the water had risen about two and a half feet since I had passed before and was far above the hubs of the wheels, beyond the bellies of the mules, and we had to pull our feet in. Once or twice we nearly capsized and everyone would throw his weight on the opposite side of the wagon to bring it back to normal.

Finally, we arrived and six of us climbed into Mr. Thomen's "Whoopie" (Oklahoman for Ford - when a Lizzie hits a bump on the road, you may notice that the most natural thing and usual exclamation of people in the back seat who bounce up in the air is "whoopie!") and came back to use the facilities, then lunch.

This afternoon I rested a little and then went out again. Four of the engineers were totally cut off - rafts had to be built for them to reach land. One fell in and swam. Then back to town - the whole south and extreme western end is completely under water. We went west and I climbed up upon the top of some freight cars with Bryce and looked it over. The Midland Railway Depot was under about three feet of water and the dam and reservoir had overflowed, a lovely little "whoopie" stood on an elevation, tied to a telegraph pole, hen coops, house tops, barns, all floated along in the swiftly moving dark grayish brown mill race.

Now, it is pouring again - rain, rain, rain. Whether or not we will go under water I am unaware. But this much you know, dearest, even if you do not get this letter, and we are wiped out - I love you, will always love you. I don't think there's much chance - but there have been affairs like that - but you've been more than life to me - you're the best and only pal I've ever had and I love you.

I don't believe this rain will ever stop.

(Later by several hours)

Well, it did stop, and rain washed, fresh and sparkling stars gleam pitifully down on wagon loads of dazed numb people, beds, ill-assorted articles of furniture, small drowsy children weeping without being aware of the reason.

It must be awful to see the house, so small, that you had furnished, lived in, loved in,  whose every nook and cranny were dear and familiar stand bravely against the flood for a few minutes, sway, start adrift, and crash to smithereens against some firmer object. I've seen so many little frame houses do that today, and as long as I live, I'll never forget the refugees I've seen. When, at the beginning of the world war, Southern England was invaded by the homeless Belgians, I have seen eyes and similar stares.

I saw one little boy, holding a pet rabbit tight in his arms, tears rolling down his face, with a grin stretched from ear to ear. He had just rescued the little beast from a watery grave.

The report just came in that the construction office where I was this morning is completely under water. Three engineers are trapped like rats in the warehouse, two more on a knoll opposite. They have sent them food by flimsy cockleshells of boats and offered to take them back to land, but they are afraid to risk the swirling mill race, and prefer to remain perched for the night on the hill.

Red Miller, my crazy, homely Texan, proved to be just the game true sport I thought him to be - he swam the mill race to those fools three times there and three times back, as messenger boy, then collapsed. Brave kid.

And all because those asinine men wanted to take pictures of each other wading about in the water in high boots - they got caught! "Lord, what fools these mortals be!"

As always, with love, Dollie

(According to historical records, nearly four inches of rain fell in the area in a period of 24 hours. There was major destruction and disruption of services, including the mail. Most residents put their lives on hold until the waters receded.)

ANGELS COULD DO NO MORE

June 21, 1923
Arkansas City, Kansas

My Dearest:

Last night, I went to a barnstorming company play and then took a walk with Bryce, to find on my return, a thick letter from you.

Oh my dear! Tenderness refuses to be expressed, endearments are futile. There was never a phrase loving enough to apply to you.

Child, never, never be afraid of losing my esteem and love, my emotional outbursts. Why, they're part of you, dear - they're scraps of my Hazel that I treasure more than untold gold. Do not leash yourself before others who cannot understand. Tell me everything. I know the feeling, I understand, and love.

Last night I prayed that I might be worthy of your love, and always keep it, for life would be empty and hollow without it. And, I cried, Hazel, cried tears of impotence and longing, helplessness and yearning. I wanted so to be with you, to try humbly to make up the love you need.

(In her own hand)

> Last night I prayed that I
> might be worthy of your love — and
> always keep it for life would be
> empty and hollow without it. And
> I cried, Hazel, cried tears of impotence
> and longing, helplessness and yearning.
> I wanted so to be with you, to try
> humbly to make up the love you need.

Don't hate me for what I'm going to say, but I realized that your mother cared for you in the way you say long ago. And I tried a little to make up for it. Did I help? Do I help, at all?

I want you to know, as you surely must, that I have always felt towards you a tenderness that I have felt for no other being. A vague wanting to shield, to help, to love - oh, it's indefinable, but, you understand.

You have done your duty, you have been everything a daughter should - unselfish, self-sacrificing, self-effacing. And, I respect you above all people for it. Perhaps I wouldn't care so much about you if you hadn't been. Ah, but I would! For you're you, and that is the answer to any question.

The cowboy's epitaph fits you to perfection: "You done your damndest. Angels could do no more."

Now for the questions. First: I don't want you to come to me out here for the simple reason that I want to come back.

Second: You couldn't get work here. There being so little demand for it. Only experienced people are employed.

I can only obtain positions as a substitute very irregularly, and then due to Betty's influence, who, though she cannot fully comprehend our friendship ("There was never a love like ours"), in a way, understands how much I long to come back, for she too has a pal.

 Mother can't give me my fare, for buying this Hup

(Hupmobile) has put the family exchequer on the blink. And that's that.

But every penny that I get from the positions Betty helps me to procure is going to be saved, to come back to you, my dearest.

And, if you could hold on to some money to help me - well, pride, independence, self-reliance would all be discarded for I love you too well to be selfish enough to pamper a whim instead of returning.

Darling, you must not marry Mac (Harold McClary) yet. Time - God - there are years and years for you to be married in, and I ask only a little part of your life. Perhaps I am still being selfish - I can't help it - I want you to help me to get back. Oh, I can't stay when every waking and sleeping thought demands fulfillment of my desire to return. Help me dear, write to me more often - just as freely - whatever you say or do can never lessen my love.

Stick it out for my sake, sweets. If you come out here we'll never get enough money to get us both home, whereas, if we both try, staying where you are - why I should be back to you soon (but it won't be soon enough for me, each day's one day too much).

Remember that I would do anything for you - give my heart's blood for you - that phrase seems extravagant but it isn't. It's what I feel! I would!

And, dearest of girls, if it does help you at all, I'll write to you every day - and I wish you'd write me more frequently. The letter I got last night was the first for a week.

This letter goes special delivery!

Please try your very damndest to see if you can't raise some money to help me to come back and know that I'm working and praying my goddamndest to do so.

Your own, Dollie

(Author's note: Dollie's friend Hazel had been seeing Harold Benjamin "Mac" McClary, for over a year when they decided to marry October 29, 1924, about a year and a half after Dollie's plea not to. Mac had attended the University of Pennsylvania but dropped out in his fourth year after he learned his parents refinanced the house to pay his tuition. He got a job with the Atlantic Richfield Oil Company in the Philadelphia office. It's possible that in his travels with his job he was able to visit Dollie, also working in an office of an oil company. Since Hazel and Dollie were friends it was natural Mac may have spent time with Dollie.)

THE CHERRY TREES FLAUNT GREEN PLUMES BESIDE THE WINDOWS

June 27, 1923
Arkansas City, Kansas

My Dearest Hazel:

(From the field office, mid- afternoon)
Don't know whether this will last or not, but
prayers do seem to be answered some time, and
here little Dollie is slaving away like a mule,

save for the odd moments when she types a bit to Hazel or sneaks out to catch a drag with Red Miller.

Peculiar building this, all clean fresh pine, and new desks, with young alert people all merrily digging in. Personally, I don't give a tinker's damn for any of ´em – save for Red and Thomen and a chap named Horn. But there's a hot breeze blowing across the sand, the cherry trees flaunt green plumes beside the windows, and as I'm beside the open door, I can look out and see the trams and tractors transforming this sandy waste into a place of business. Two weeks ago, muddy water flowed around and in this very building, and Horn and Thomen and several others were imprisoned in it. Now, the sun shines warmly down, the sand whirls in miniature tornadoes, Horn sits across the way, stroking his slick black hair and laughing at some timeworn jest. Thomen stands outside the door flicking cigarette ashes at me, sticking his tongue out and blowing cigarette smoke in my general direction to taunt me. What a difference a few weeks will make! Think – I may soon be back with you. Atta girl! And then, ah, won't we have a hell of a time!

(A few days later) I went for a walk last night and had a rather stupid time generally.

Since I kissed Herbert on top of his curly head, he has avoided me as the plague. I believe he mistrusts my intentions, which I venture to state are perfectly honorable. Poor boy, being pursued by a city slicker.

I've taken two baths this morning, cold, but the perspiration beads my pallid brow, and I feel as though I were in a Turkish bath.

We're going over to have dinner with the Johnson's shortly. It sounds interesting, save for the fact that I have lost my appetite these hot days.

Child, child dear – my only thought – the thing I live for echoes through my brain – I'm going back, back to my love, my life – soon, ah, soon! God, God help me!

(Several hours later) Well, we ate and there the entire Johnson family and ours filed into the Hup and Roy Webber's Mercer. I got into the latter as Bob always pokes along, and believe me, we passed everything on the road. Just out through Winfield and Oxford but I collected enough grime on my noble physiognomy in which to plant potatoes.

Now I'm home again, it's only eight thirty – I have no date, no Hazel – nothing. But it won't be long now, and I'll be back again, a la proverbial bad penny.

I'm going to post this now, as all the places to buy stamps close at nine.

So, with all the love I am capable of, I am,

Your Dollie

THREATS FROM THE KLAN

July 7, 1923
Arkansas City, Kansas

Dearest of all:

Things have been happening with a vengeance. I'll start at the beginning.

Oh, well, last night I had a date with the St. Louis boy and was told we were the best looking pair. There, that's right, laugh, darn you. But Mark had on a clever tie, a blue sack coat, white linen knickers. He's about six foot, red headed, regular features and very blue eyes. I wore a little tan hat and my Paisley dress. He dances wonderfully, and there are no illusions whatever – he, knowing that I am not serious, is playing the part as best he can after you, my pal. Everything went along nicely between us. But wait!

Now the bloody details of the night – let me begin properly.

The man in the hat asked me to wear a peculiar signet ring of his as a token that whenever he might blow into town, he'd be able to have a date. You remember of my speaking of Luke Harris. Well, yesterday I met him and he laughingly confiscated the ring. I so rarely wear jewelry that I forgot he had it until today, but I couldn't call him because he's married and his wife might answer the phone. Tonight, however, I made a pledge and told myself that I was going to bed early, but when Mark and Allen drove up in an overpowering Cadillac, I cast my resolution to the wind and sallied forth. It was well worth it – the sky was that faint grayish pink scattered with stars that soothes and calms, and the wind in my face was as a benediction. Mark has the gift of silence, and we didn't speak until the car pulled up on the prairie. Then the boys drank some liquor and I smoked a cigarette or two and thought of you.

Then, very suddenly, horribly, soundlessly, white figures seemed to rise from the ground, hemming us all in a silent, cruel,

 ghastly circle that narrowed relentlessly. I realized that it was the Ku Klux Klan and that they had probably thought us neckers, thus rating us a flogging. I knew that any escape was impossible. We were all sitting on the running board, the engine was dead. The other girl was scared and so was I.

A beastly wailing sound cut the night like a knife but I stuck to my cigarette while seeking inspiration. Things blurred a bit, I was chuckling to myself.

Mark was digging for his automatic and muttering curses. Allen was holding the other girl, a limp little bundle, in his arms. And me, dragging on the almost extinguished butt while a mob of idiots in none too clean nightshirts played at being stern destroyers of youthful and natural indiscretions. A light flashed in my face. A hand roughly pulled me to my feet, while others held Mark.

We were all questioned. Instinctively I ducked my head at the blaze of light and flung it back, for I was ashamed of none of my actions. Instantly my arm was released, the Klansman threw his arm up before his face, but before he switched off his light I recognized the ring as the one the man in the hat had given me.

Things kind of died down after that. A few questions or so, and my Klansman in a muffled voice saying "Get in the car. Go!"

But I knew him. It was Luke Harris, and I think he must like me a little bit.

Mark swore all the way home. He had wanted to fight, but the girl wept and I hated her, for she was a coward!

But Luke, Luke a Klansman? That's a laugh. I can't tell anyone, but you, about this. The affair must he hushed up, but now, sweets, it's one-thirty and I am awfully, awfully tired.

Goodnight, my dearest.
Dollie

I'LL COME BACK TO YOU

Thursday, July 19, 1923
Arkansas City, Kansas

Dear Hazel:

Last night I saw Mark, but I cut him deliberately, so while I was catching a Coca-Cola he sent me a note by the boy, asking me to do him the favor I once asked of him- namely go to hell. Whereupon I sent him one in return saying I was flattered by his invitation but that I hadn't had the slightest desire for his company, either, in this world or the next.

So by tacit agreement this morning, the Irish in us compelled a somewhat impudent grin on my face, and a wry one on his, and we laughed, shook hands and were pals. But it was good-bye, for he leaves tonight for the head office. I'm sorry, because he was rather a decent sort. Said he, "If I wrote you Dollie, would I get an answer?" Poor old kid!

Oh, God, it's hot, hot, hot! I positively cook, and swelter in my own sweat. I bathe and cover myself with talcum, to emerge with a pale coating of paste on my face instead of powder. It's plum hell. But they say it stays this way for about a month and then gets worse! Why it's 110 degrees in my room, and not a breath of wind; just gulping in great mouthfuls of hot fetid air.

The family is arguing again – oh, God and in such weather.

Where I stopped last night, and as my train of thought has been completely broken, must go on with what happened later.

Peg and I went down to the Town Thriller, and saw a wrestling match. Yelled myself hoarse, squashed young Barclay's new Panama, and my feet being on the bench in front of me – nearly kicked holes in the man's back who sat before me.

At about nine thirty we started home and had gone about two blocks when a Dodge coupe stopped, a decent looking boy in linen knickers hopped out and taking off his straw hat (I noticed it had a Princeton band) asked if he might drive us home. I climbed in first, saying- "Not home." So we drove up and down the main drag and I learned he came from Princeton, more recently from Chicago, that his Dad owned the next biggest refinery to the Roxana in town, that he is blond and blue eyed similar to Gibbie and an irresistible flirt. He tried to ditch Peg, and stopped his car at Fifth Avenue and Summit to light a match for my cigarette, suspending traffic, leaving us with a long trail of cars in our wake, and the angry curses of drivers floating about us. He told little risqué border stories, "not quite the proper thing," yet, not the sort to cause offense. In fact, he was delightful, just the sort of man you'd like, and I wished so that you were there, and not Peg who missed the point of half his stories and all his glances. Of course, I realize that he is merely a flirt - a Princetonian proper, but he was amusing, deferential and respectful, more so than many men I've met for a long time, so now after I wash my neck, comb my hair, put on a clean shirtwaist, sweater and skirt "I'm going out to meet him for another ride of which I'll tell you tomorrow.

I pray he isn't a beast, but so many men are!

Dearest, you have all my heart no matter how I flirt or trifle, and the thought that is always with me is, "I'm going back to her!"

Dollie

NEVER BE ASHAMED OF EMOTION

August 23, 1923
Arkansas City, Kansas

Sweets:

Last night, Dollie arrayed herself in raiment – namely that lemon satin, with black bows at wrists and neck, lemon head band, silver slippers and stockings, towed by a nice blonde curly-haired boy from Kansas University and went out about five miles to an open air dance. It really wasn't bad – good floor, good imported orchestra. I met some very nice looking boys and girls – but, delight my soul – this western hospitality stuff is a dead letter. My dances were all taken, but I think more because of the fact that I was a "new girl" and an easterner, than because I was me. But I have never been so unhappy that I decided one evening at least should be mine again – one evening of laughter. So I mocked everyone, my date, the girls, the men, myself. They played *Dearest* and just as they started, the dynamo or something electrical gave out and all the lights went out. I haven't described the floor to you – hidden in a grove of trees, with three rows of young saplings rising through the floor.

A silver half-moon festooned the sky and when they played *Dearest* (my name for you) I thought of Mac and you, how you both loved it so. And so I closed my eyes and rested my head on my date's shoulder. He seemed a sympathetic soul, for he danced silently and held me gently in his arms, only saying "It will be all right. Buck up." Closing my eyes I felt the breeze play on my hot face, the tender sweep of the young leaves through my hair, and in spite of all brave resolutions, one big, gasping, hurtful sob tore its way up from my heart. Herbert only held me tight for a minute, saying "There my dear, there." He was the first man to comfort me. I always seem to be a binder of wounds.

I got in at one thirty, and as I ran up the steps I thought how decent Herbert had been – and caught his face between my hands and dropped a light kiss on his blonde hair. Then dashed into the house.

(Next day) Now I'm going up to see Betty at the office to ask if she can't give me something to do "pronto." I'll write the results later.

(An hour later) I took your letter up and read as much as I saw fit to Betty and we talked of you and her pal, Grace. It seems Grace will be coming down soon, and Betty said, after she heard what you said, she said, "Try Dollie, you've got to go back to her."

Me? Yes, yes, you fool, but where am I going to get the money?

Pause.

Betty – slowly, meditatively – "Well, I'll help you, and Grace will help you, and I'll try to get you some regular work – I don't think I can, but I'll try." Then Betty says her brother-in-law might let her have some cash. "I'll help you with clothes, Grace and my brother-in-law will help you with money. We must get you back to her!"

Isn't that incredible? Just because she has a pal? It's a great company and I have faithful friends. I'm thinking that the milk of human kindness is so sweet and warm. Ah, my

dearest, you must wait for me now. No matter
how tempted you may be when Mac asks you to
go to him and things are wrong – people are
querulous and demanding – sneak off to your
room, light a cigarette, curse until exhausted
and write to me.

(In her own hand)

As an antidote, it's perfect. I've tried it.

By the way, send my knickers soon or I
won't have a chance to wear them here. And, if

you can manage it, smuggle me in a couple of decks of Camels or Benson & Hedges, for supplies are running low, and I can't buy more when I'm saving.

And, dearest, remember, my affection not being easily gained, is just as hard to lose. Never be ashamed of emotion. If genuine, it is always worthy.

Dear, I'll come back soon, soon.
Still, Your Dollie

BOBBED-HAIRED DOLLIE

September 20, 1923
Arkansas City, Kansas

Hazel mine:

This morning I received a totally
unexpected and cheery letter from Ma. It was
just what I needed for I've been so damned
sorry for me for a couple of days that I can't see
straight. But upon receipt of the note I
abandoned all thought of going into the yard in
order to devour worms, either the slick or
woolly kind, for there was so much reassurance
and niceness condensed in that one note. So
much sweetness was a delight. Mac's the same
dear old "blarneyer" that I knew, bless him,
and I hope to God the three of us will soon be

together where you can blissfully utter
idealisms and I'll do my damnedest to shatter in
with cynicism's I scarcely believe myself.

Damn it, Hazel, this is no place for me!
When Mac and you get married there must be a
"reserved" seat for me by your fireside and
Mac and I will smoke each other's cigarettes
and (as you'll be his wife and lawful property),
he may once in a while allow you one.

So long as I am certain of the love of you
both I don't give a damn for anything else.
See? Don't you feel flattered? Well you should.
What effect has my second letter had on Mac?

You know, I had started to grow my hair
and it was quite long. I did it up in a lot of trick
twirls that completely backed the fair hurricane
Gloria off the map. The problem is I couldn't
stand it and I looked too dignified. So I'm still

the bobbed-haired Dollie. Keep yours short,
too, sweets. Won't you?

I've got a blinding headache, but I can't
leave the office, so I'm sitting, smoking all the
boss's cigarettes. He told me the other day, he
rather have me smoke at my desk than sneak
out behind the office and corrupt the engineers.
So I've taken him at his word.

For the last few weeks we've had only
rain but today the sulky sun is shining.

Shep and I rode out here at noon in his
Essex and at one spot that was particularly
muddy, turned completely around. He is a
confident driver though sometimes I'm afraid
his confidence is misplaced.

This letter is getting frightful. I'll stop
and write more tomorrow. Dear, if you could

find the time to write more frequently, please do. Your letters mean so much.

Your Dollie

A VISIT FROM MOTHER

October 19, 1923
Arkansas City, Kansas

My girl –

Your note arrived today, so I am answering it promptly as possible. You see, dear they forwarded it from the office to my home address.

I've been having quite a time with Mother and feel like a particularly dirty dog. The scourge of the earth but, nonetheless, I'm going to come back – and that's that! You wouldn't write to me again after you receive this. On Tuesday or Wednesday of next week I'm taking off for God's country. Please excuse the assorted writing.

Heard from Ross again but haven't heard from Tex for almost a month. There are no visible marks of grief.

Sorry dear that I haven't written. I've had my hands pretty full running around with Mother. Lou's been in evidence quite a bit.

By the way, I gave the office boy a wire to send to you, and sent a special delivery the same day acknowledging receipt of the money. Didn't you receive them?

I tried to write yesterday, but there seems to be so much to do.

Child dear, if only you knew how fussed I am! I do the daftest things. I look blank and poppy-eyed if anyone says "Boo!" to me.

Save the Princeton, lad's letter for me, and I'll try to scratch out a note to you before I leave.

Yours shortly, Dollie

DOLLIE GETS MARRIED

May 21, 1926
Ardmore, Oklahoma

Dear Hazel:

I never replied to your card because —
well, somehow, I've been a poor correspondent
of late.

Probably, you'll have connected the name
on the envelope with me and know that I've
married, last Tuesday. I've known Joe for only
six weeks but strangely enough, I've always
thought I would marry quickly, like a man
committing suicide, on the impulse of the
moment. I love him, Hazel. He's six foot one,
very dark, brown eyed, nice to look at, has a
sense of humor, a Ford coupe, and most

importantly, my love. He has been educated at the ministry, but backslid on reading the infidel authors and studied piano at MacPhail Center for Music in Minneapolis. He's a marvelous musician. He has a pronounced taste for James Branch Cabell, Anatole France, Knut Hamsun – books he loves and has in quantities. We've no money, but that doesn't count. We'll muddle through somehow.

Hazel, I never knew I could care as much for anyone. I'm utterly pleased and I can't quite talk about it. We love each other so very much.

Won't you write and tell me that you
hope this will last? If it doesn't, I want to die.

My love to Mac and all – and you.

Dollie

(Author's note: The newspaper spells Dollie's
last name as Clark. Dollie always used Clarke.)

AN IMPOSSIBLY IDYLLIC LITTLE WHITE HOUSE

May 31, 1926
Ardmore, Oklahoma

Dear Hazel:

Perhaps I was abrupt, but so was my marriage. You see, I only knew Joe for six weeks and then we came to the conclusion that there was no use in being so uselessly and needlessly separated. And so we were married, very quietly and circumspectly, with two of Joe's friends as our witnesses, at their house.

Karl Tietgens and his wife are interesting people. He, a German, about 45, tall and blonde and Prussian. She is a violinist of ability; small and sharp and dark, with a face that might have been carved in tiny yellowed ivory.

And (did I tell you?) I lost my voice during the ceremony and sputtered and waved my hands in the mildly reproachful clergyman's face.

Mother took it badly. She would, you know, because I've been a constant companion to her these last two years, and now she misses me. But, don't you know, there's no change in the feelings towards Mother? I'll always care for her, but she tries to convince herself that I won't. It hurts me, rather a great deal. And, what can I do?

Joe is a superb pianist. But he has grown disgusted with the art. A phase, I think. I know little of music, but sometimes he plays for me - and it is rather marvelous. He only plays popular music on his banjo, and sings in a good baritone. He finds working for an oil company more lucrative than art in Oklahoma. He is an Oklahoman by birth, but rather cosmopolitan.

He is six foot one, dark brown eyed, good to look at, splendid build, weighs, I think, 185 pounds, talks well, reads all the books I like to read, and has a sense of humor. I've tried not to rhapsodize, and to be lucid.

But, oh, it's hard to be sane. We live in an impossibly idyllic little white house, with a picket fence, and great crimson roses dripping from the trellises. And at night a great musical comedy, golden moon tears itself from the arms of the silent trees to shine for us, as we sit on the porch, Joe at my feet, his dear dark head against my knee, and our cigarettes glowing, turn circles of fire.

And I had not known that life could be so very dear. I love. I am loved. We're young. The gods are kind. Too kind. Sometimes I fear that they may become jealous of my happiness.

Hazel, don't ask me to become sensible now. It's asking too much of me. Soon, very soon, I'll write again, discussing the rest of your questions. Joe wanted to thank you for your telegram. He doesn't know yet that I've heard from you again. Please thank Mac for us.

Here's my love,
Dollie

THE RELATIONSHIP
COOLS

August 23, 1926
Ardmore, Oklahoma

My Dear Hazel:

Now I am quite positive that I replied to
your nice telegram with a letter after our
marriage and therefore, feel justified in the
anger which consumes me at your prolonged
silence. Somehow, though perhaps it may have
seemed a discreet and kind thing to do, not
writing, a sort of "Oh leave them alone, they
would really rather be, they're so newly wed." I
would have much appreciated a letter from you.

And I must tell you that I believe myself
to be incurably married. You know how often

I've cried "Wolf!" But this – well, this astounds even me. I'm afraid I love not wisely, but to well, but I know that it's a reciprocal affair, and what care I? Life's too short, and Heaven seems to preclude all the folly of which I am still capable, I find. In fact, I'm just so damned happy that I'm positive something awful will happen, because the gods will grow jealous of me.

Mother is more reconciled now, and Gerry has just ended a three-week visit with us. I no longer feel like the family pariah. It's rather awful having your mother treating you as though you had committed all the sins in the Decalogue, merely because you have married. Though doubtless you will remember all my protestations against the state of holy matrimony. So much had I talked on the matter to the family, that they and even I were fully convinced that I was destined for a life as an old maid, and when I did get married, on three-days-notice, and only knowing Joe for a month, you may imagine the tears and warnings with which the event was hailed. But we've all life before us, Hazel, and we're young, both of us just twenty one.

Today we were really extravagant. We've not much money, you know, but we both love music so, and we bought an orthophonic Victrola, and turned our old one in. It's a beauty, and has a lovely tone, and after all, "man does not live by bread alone." You remember the oft quoted sentence – "Had I two loaves of bread, one I would exchange for white hyacinths?" We're both that way, and I suppose we will eventually land in the gutter, with tin cups and eye shades, a little dog leading us as we whine, "Please help the blind."

I just finished reading Anatole France's last book, or rather the notes he had compiled towards it – "Under the Roses." It's a series of dialogues and epigrams and observations, similar to "The Garden of Epicurus" by the same author. Also "Brawnyman" by James Stevens, author of those Paul Bunyan things which are very good. "Brawnyman," alas is a frightful flop.

I will write no more, because I feel righteously indignant, and that it is your turn to write to me. Please give my love to Mac, and I know Joe would join me, were he in (which he isn't) in sending a great quantity to yourself. I'm off.

Ever, Dollie

(Author's note: There isn't another letter on file until 1938. Does it mean there was a falling out between the friends? In the meantime Dollie's daughter Ann was born in 1927.)

Hazel McClary, 1930

HURT FEELINGS, NURSING MOTHER

September 3, 1938
Oklahoma City, Oklahoma

Dear Hazel:

I was most happy to have your letter, and rather surprised by the gist of the comments, for although in closing you said you "Didn't mind at all," which is gracious of you, I feel your muster or you would not have written so emphatically. I am sorry I blundered so, but I am not sure just how I offended. I make a wholesale apology to cover all errors of both omission and commission.

I thought Mrs. Roberts your personal friend – an assumption, as you say, but rather a natural one since I judged from the text of your letter, although as you also said, I have no knowledge of your relations with her. If – to quote you again – my thank you note to her was "impossible," I am quite sorry nevertheless, since it was written with the utmost sincerity, I feel you are a trifle harsh. Thinking her your friend, and she having inscribed the book in such a friendly manner, it was natural to think she had sent the book to me and to not have written her my thanks would have been crass. It appalls me that my note appeared to you to be "stiff and condescending," for it was not meant so, but thank you notes to people whom you have not met are inclined to be stilted and trite despite those good intentions. I am embarrassed you think I made comparisons between my poor poems and Mrs. Roberts' works – I merely sought to find a common ground where we could meet when I commented on writing to her.

I did think I thanked you for sending the book, and am upset to think you believe I did not appreciate the kindness of your having sent it. Believe me I was pleased at your having thought of me. I did not know you intended me to give the book to Ann, because it had been inscribed to me. I thought it was a gift to me and I was very happy to have it. Also, I have enjoyed the verses – if I did not say so before it was because in observing one amenity, that of writing promptly, I neglected another – that of reading the book before I wrote.

Ann took off her brace the day before yesterday and today we paid a visit to the good doctor, and she can go without it from now on. It is a great happiness to all of us to see her up and around again. She enrolled in junior high school this morning, and now the next thing is for Mother to start sewing her school trousseau. I have made practically all my own winter wardrobe already – woolens, and with the weather so hot it has been a job. I also made one brown wool street dress, one green wool street dress, and one thin black wool afternoon dress. I have a tweed suit from last year, three-piece, and a black broadcloth suit. I need a new purse and another pair of gloves and I am all right. I may make myself a heavy winter coat later; I can't bear to think of any more sewing just now.

It is, as you say, difficult for you to visualize Ann, if you have not seen her. She is about four feet three inches, weighs eighty-five pounds; correct for her age. She is well formed, her skin is very fair and she is definitely blonde. She has worn her hair long, to her shoulders, for some years, but we were compelled to give her a boy's haircut when she was in the hospital. Her eyes are blue, she has a wide, thin-lipped mouth and a snub nose. Her hands and feet are large – her feet are my greatest expense, her foot being extremely narrow and necessitating expensive shoes. Her color is good, she usually has rosy cheeks, and in spite of the summer in the cast and brace, she has kept out in the air so that she is tanned like an Indian. By ordinary standards, when her back isn't broken, she is very active, and even still has time to have large and rather startling zoological exhibits.

At present we are rather low, having only a jarful of ants (she keeps them in earth in a half-gallon jar, to watch their habits). A wooden box, screened of course, contains several varieties of grasshoppers. Another wooden box, also screened, contains a pair of praying mantis, plus a washtub full of water in which lives a disgruntled and surly bullhead catfish. Besides these are four kittens and their mother, the Irish setter, and a toad named Edgar.

We have everything from snapping turtles on. She has a decided bent for animals, and at present her ambition is to grow up and study medicine, but has variously wished to be a movie star, an opera singer, and artist, a dress designer and a trapeze performer. I am not regarding the situation with much hope.

I had a portrait – a photo, I mean – made with Ann this spring, and am having some more copies made. If you care for it, I'll send you one.

I am truly sorry that you seemed to think me slighting or careless or whatever you did think in regard to the book. I do thank you for it, and for having thought of me. It was most good of you. If I seemed to be neglectful – think of how busy I have been this summer, and I know you will understand.

Again, thanks for your letter and for the book also.

Most sincerely,
Dollie

P.S. Pardon friend – I'm sticking in a poem of mine. I thought you might like to see. Incidentally, this is no comparison intended with Mrs. Roberts' poems. I know mine can't stand comparison, poor thing!

NURSING MOTHER

A woman who has born a son
Feels her task is nearly done.
She sits and watches as he takes

Greedy gulps of life, and aches
Because he'll go beyond recall
And have no need of her at all.
With bone and muscle, blood and nerve
She makes him hers, beyond the curve
Of her white breast, secretive brow
Conceals him from her, even now.
The lines about her mouth are grim
Wondering what may come to him
Now in the circle of her arm.
From sudden death, from war's alarm
She would protect him even when
He grows, as babies grow, to men.
From human ills which flesh may fret
She would provide an amulet,
From broken faith, from poverty
Of purse and spirit she would free
Her son and she would give him such
Wisdom that the wintry touch
Of pain should leave him undistressed
Full fed, his lips have left her breast,
His round, small head begins to nod.
She blinks weak tears away, "Please
God."

I'M HAPPY

April 16, 1939
Oklahoma City, Oklahoma

Dear Hazel:

I received your card a few weeks ago, and I am glad that you are having a grand time galloping around.

You asked if I had ceased writing letters, and indeed I have not – but, "Mr. Pot" who are you to inquire? The last time you wrote, quoth Mr. Kettle, was somewhere around October (last year). And you must admit that postcards don't nourish correspondence as well as letters do.

I think spring has come to Oklahoma, but one is never sure. We've had plum, cherry and pear and peach trees in swirls of bloom, but we've also had freezes, and thick yellow dust storms, and tornados in the northwestern portion of the state. Besides, there is a hallowed saying here – only fools and newcomers prophesy Oklahoma weather.

But, I may say cautiously, the rosebushes are budded. I have iris, hyacinth and violets blooming and the jonquils and daffodils have bloomed, been cut and decorated the tables. The grass is green, and this afternoon I'm going to take the lawnmower out for its first foray of the year.

My vegetable garden has yielded radishes and scallions already, and the peas, beans, potatoes and spinach and carrots and corn are poking up as well. My vegetable garden is a

manifestation of the earth's renewal of itself —
so hard it was last year, with caked soil and salt
water, it was like plowing up the highway. But
this year it is mulching and looks well.

We have five new kittens, three grey and
two whites, and they are beginning to open little
liquid diamond shaped eyes. The dogs
gloriously hunt imagined rabbits all the day,
instead of sitting, shivering on haunches that
shrink upward from the ground.

We have had the Turtle (small boat) I
repainted and a new motor installed and Joe's
trying it out down in the Kiamichi this
weekend, on Mountain Fork River. I went
fishing for the first time since Ann was hurt. I
went to Silver Lake, but caught only one
miserable three-inch bass. Too cold; too much
rain.

 I'm enclosing a picture of Ann, I have none of myself. Soon I'll have some perhaps. Ann's in wonderful shape, an attestation to the elasticity of youth. She is twelve now, in a strong adolescence and I am very happy in her recovery and the companionship we share.

I'm better, too, although I did have a rather nasty time around the Christmas season. Hospitals are never much fun, especially when you are snatched out of the festival preparations to have to lie, packed in hot packs, thinking of all you have to do when you get out. However, everyone was grand and kind, and my nurses swell, and I'm all right now, so it doesn't matter.

This is really a note, which you might answer, and then I'll write a better one, I hope.

Hope you are well.

Love, Dorothy

(Note: This is the first time Dollie referred to herself as Dorothy.)

YEAR'S AT SPRING

In her April 16, 1939 note Dollie included the following verse with a short note:

YEAR'S AT SPRING

Along each hill
The petalled snow
Of dogwood and
The rebud blow,
And in the small
Brook's quickened gait
Spring becomes
Articulate.
Arms locked, the boys
And Girls go walking,
In silences more
Sweet than talking.
Do not shake
Your head, recall
How very soon
It will be fall.

Dollie's note:

I've done several more things of the jingle type, and seem to have pretty fair luck with them.

Yes, you'd probably think me changed. I don't yearn so much for the old things; I'm rather happy as I am, although we're not wealthy and have to make a bow to compromise fairly constantly. Yet, I've good companions, a child who interests and amuses me, and a nice husband. That's a lot, isn't it? And I'm healthy and strong. And, I enjoy being alive. So my lot doesn't bore me, and even if I am somewhat circumscribed, I'm happy.

I must stop. Do write again.
Love, Dorothy

THE BUSINESS OF POVERTY

March 6, 1941
Choctaw, Oklahoma

Dear Hazel:

I did write to you, when I heard from you of your loss, and am wondering whether I perhaps addressed it wrongly, since you do not seemed to have received it. Believe me I am very sorry about that which I know must be an ever present grief to you. It is the kind of thing that is hard to express, but my sympathy for you is very real.

In my letter, too, I told you of Joe's company blowing up, and our subsequent decision to have one good fishing trip before we starved to death, which we damn near had, and then settled down to the business of poverty. We moved out here from town, not being able to afford the up keep of our house there, which was rather expensive, and took the little matchbox of a house, not modern, with ten acres of ground. Joe was without work for more than six months, and as we have merrily spent every cent of our income always, we have been nibbling the edges very closely. Now, he has a stop-gap sort of job which brings in enough to scrape by with – it's not his type of work, and is hard work, too, but he doesn't seem to object for he's learning something in the process.

I have this little four-room house to take care of, and Arvo resides (sleeps) in a little room in the rear-end of the garage. We came here in the middle of the summer when everything was lush and lovely – now it's black and bitter and, at the present, time, since we have a four-month old pup, the yard looks like that of a "poor trash" house. We have no gas, electricity or running water, but we have a big fireplace and burn wood. There is a pump in the back yard, and I traded off my heart's darling (my practically new, white stove) for a kerosene kitchen range. We burn kerosene lamps and you would be surprised how little it takes to live, and enjoy yourself.

I canned everything the country offered last summer, knowing that we'd be broke this winter. I put up all sorts of vegetables, about six hundred quarts all told. I did the jellies and jams separately. I canned peaches, pears, apple sauce, rhubarb, asparagus, tomatoes, green beans, summer squash, plums, greens, new potatoes, corn, okra, soup vegetables, beets, relishes and pickles. I also put up plum, apple and blackberry jelly; peach, pear and strawberry preserves – ad nausea.

I'm sorry I did not send cards at Christmas – we didn't send any, for one thing or another; I was flat on my back with the flu.

You speak of not writing – dear Hazel – I have been busy. My correspondence naturally suffers. The boys leave for town in the mornings at seven and I'm alone then, when Ann leaves at eight for school, until five at night. I have pigs to feed, chickens to feed and water, the house to do, wood to carry in, water to draw, bread to bake and a thousand and one other things to do each day. I have over fifty chickens, pullets, that I raised from two-days old, and I have to attend to them thoroughly – even to cleaning their coop. I have raised some pigs, and butchered two already, made sausage and canned it. I cured sides and shoulders and made hams. It's nothing to brag about because most farm women do the same, but it's plenty for me. Because Joe isn't a farmer and around to lend a hand when I need it, I do most of the work here solo. Sundays he helps me do things and we have lots of fun, go rabbit hunting or puddle-ducking , then frequently dropping in town for concerts. We're on the highway, twelve miles out of town. My men never get home in the evening until past seven, then we read, or play a wild and lawless game of poker, or fall asleep over a paragraph, because we're all tired.

I've so little time to spare, and what I have I must use for Ann and myself. She's fourteen and becoming very clothes conscious. She's as tall as I am, and becoming quite sightly. She is even taking care of her hair and nails without prompting this year, so you see, she's growing up. I make almost all her clothing and my own, although my uniform here most days is a sweatshirt and denim britches. But I do dress when I go to town. I have a spring suit that I'm fairly busting to make. I want a torso length coat, skirt and slacks out of it – a chunk of light green wool – but, although I've had the material six weeks, I've not had time to sew it. I'm crocheting a bed spread. I've got the top pieced to a Texas Star quilt. I crocheted a luncheon set. I write a bit (have sold a couple to the most minor of the women's magazines) and have made a lot of my little costume dolls and have sold several. I get two-fifty for them. You see, I make the body, stuff it, and paint the features with watercolors, sew on the hair and then dress them to the period I wish. That's rather fun!

And of course, since every gadget I have is electric, I'm stymied here. My nine-foot Norge (refrigerator) makes a good storage space. I let Mrs. Mac have my vacuum and I am trading off my washer to her in exchange for hers, to which a gasoline motor can be attached. I traded my electric sewing machine for her treadle machine. I even let Eve take my toaster, mixer and waffle iron, since they were just gathering dust. Washing for four on a rub board isn't easy work. I had to buy a gasoline iron also.

But I can't remember when I had so much fun. I get up at five thirty, and work hard until six in the evening, then crochet or read after the rest of the family have gone off to bed. I've been reading quite a bit, get about six books a week from the library, and I'm just reading John Masefield's Basilissa (published in 1940), about the Empress Theodora, who always interested me.

As the spring comes, I shall be busier still, for there will be so much yard work. I shall have a large vegetable garden. This is a pretty place, or it will be in the spring. I have a little orchard of twenty-seven or eight trees. A little thicket of wild plums, too. I have cherry, peach, pear, apple and apricot trees, and two rows of grape vines, each about a city-block long, and five rows of blackberries of the same length. Down the drive there are rows of iris, and on the west side of the yard, a lilac fence, rose bushes, and rows and rows of more iris, of different varieties. I have planted what seeds I had from former gardens, but this year could afford no bulbs, but next year may be better. The yard is enormous here. We have two large cedars, but the rest of the trees are chiefly black jacks. Oh, there are several redbud trees, and a variety of smaller flowering shrubs, and there is a very nice fishpond where Ann dumped her fish, which immediately spawned, so we now have worlds of fishes. The fish pond draws the birds to drink, and have all varieties. We have the little linnets that are called wild canaries, red-winged blackbirds, a pair of cardinals which have wintered with us and the ever-present jays.

Everything looks very dead and dreary and messy just now, however, for it is a grey day and the yard, as I said, is littered. But in my mind's eye, I can see it when flushed by spring. So it's lovely to me. I've waited so long to move into the country and now I'm happy about it, even though the church mice do seem like bloated Plutocrats in comparison to ourselves.

We have been to whatever concerts and several things have come through Oklahoma City this year. I heard Heifetz (Jascha Heifetz was a Lithuanian-born American violinist) again, and Irene Dalis, the pianist. I also saw the Littlefield Ballet (founded in 1929). We usually go to the symphony concerts.

It's ten o'clock and the housework still confronts me, so I shall stop. Write to me. I CAN'T and WON'T call a postcard an answer to a letter. I'm sorry if I am not as regular a correspondent as I should be, but as you can see, I am a busy person.

Best Love,
Dollie

(Author's note: Dollie talks about some tragedy that her friend Hazel experienced but there is no reference to what it was. Perhaps it was the death of either Hazel's mother or father.

Dollie also refers to a man named Arvo who roomed with them. According to the 1940 census Arvo Hantula was born in 1898, in North Dakota, probably of Finnish decent.

Arvo was a classical musician and music teacher. Dollie's husband Joe was also a gifted musician and worked in the oil industry to make ends meet between musical jobs. It's possible Joe was Arvo's student. In her letters

Dollie makes reference to Joe's study of classical music. Even though they didn't have much money they still went to classical music concerts.

Arvo was college educated and remained single. Like Joe, to pay his bills, he had a job with the government. Arvo died in 1974 in Oklahoma City, Oklahoma. He was 76.

Finally, Choctaw, Oklahoma is about 20 miles east of Oklahoma City. The population in 1941 was about 300.)

DOLLIE'S REACTION TO THE WAR

June 19, 1942
Choctaw, Oklahoma

Dear Hazel:

When your letter came this morning, I was very busy riding hard on Ann, who was

making ice cream, trying to explain to the boy with the tractor that I wanted the disc run twice over the south field, doing the ironing and, while getting ready to cultivate a large patch of tomatoes,

(Hazel McClary, 1943)

pulled up my shorts and told myself that tonight I'd write a long letter. My conscience has hurt me, since I don't believe I replied to your last, and I really meant to.

You really sound tremendously busy, and I must say that I wish I had the opportunity you have to serve. I don't think I have a particular talent for organization, etc., but I do have persistence and endurances, and I don't like a job to lick me. I think you must be well fitted to hold your own where you are, and it is a field which I regard wistfully, for I should like to enter it. I've had no real training in it, however, and should have to do something about that. I've had a lot of hugger-mugger practice, and it's surprising how much a person's commonsense will do to help out in crisis. However, there's no use repining, it's impossible for me to enter the field of endeavor that you have, although I'd love it. I'm sure that you carry to it a great deal of efficiency and initiative, and I know very well you'll be a success. So, congratulations!

Philadelphia and the surrounding counties must be very lively in these times, and I'm glad to hear that the country, as a whole, is war minded. Because it still seems to me that the man in the street, here at least, is too prone to facile optimism. It is not that I do not believe in American ability and courage and ultimate success. What I deplore is the lack of realization that there are hard times ahead. As I write a low flying plane drones overhead. They fly so low over here that I could almost reach out and touch them. They're trainers, you know.

It seems odd to me that Oklahoma is one of the key states for air production, that there is still this attitude among the average citizens that this war is a far off thing. To me it is very real, harsh and horrible, and the sooner we all do something about it, the sooner it will be over. And it can't be done by conservation.

I've been, for four or five years, a Cassandra crying woe! Woe! Upon the steps of the temple, but being justified in having said so doesn't make me happier. I hate the whole beastly business of war, so who doesn't? I wish there were some way that I could do more; to help and serve.

For a while I felt rather upset about not being able to take a more active part, as I thought, but since farming has become such an essential thing, I feel I am doing my share.

We moved to this new place at the first of the year, and I like it vastly. We have one hundred fifty acres, about forty of which we cultivate, and the rest in pasture and woods. In spite of having lived on a shoe string while Joe was trying to keep our heads above water with an inferior job, and having to support various relatives at times when they were out of jobs, we somehow managed to scrape up enough for the nucleus of a little stock farm, which is mostly my responsibility now. Joe is working in the oil industry; an essential occupation, but if he were called for the draft, I would be able, I think, to carry on here by myself. I don't know whether they will take him or not. If they do, it will necessitate a long, drawn out and tedious corrective operation to overcome a physical disability.

We've had to skimp and do without a lot, but this living in the country has, I'm afraid, spoiled me for city life. And I think it has given us two of the happiest years of our lives. Too, with Ann, I think it is building into her a sense of responsibility and reason. She is fifteen now, you know, and a junior in high school. As conditions are, when she graduates, if the war's still running, she'll immediately enter nurse's training. If not, she'll take her college work and then do so, with a specific branch in mind.

As I said, Joe being at work most of the time leaves me with greater responsibility here, since we haven't been able to hire help, except tractor work for ploughing, discing and harrowing. I have some cows, calves, sows and pigs and a number of frying chickens that I'm raising. Everything isn't as I want it, in the way of equipment or housing, but it is a beginning, and since the raising of foodstuffs is so important now, I feel I'm not being a fiddler while Rome burns.

You spoke of Victory Gardens and I have more than an acre of household garden tomatoes, potatoes, corn, peas, beans and all the vegetables. I've canned quite a bit and expect to can a great deal more. Have canned cherries, beans, peas and shall have peaches to can next week. I have about four trees all ripening at one fell swoop. I will market some. I do all the gardening myself of course, since Joe works such ghastly hours. Every once in a while he has some days off, and then we all work like killing snakes, doing the work I can't accomplish by myself or with Ann's aid. We have about twenty acres of corn, and most of the rest in cane and peanuts. The government wants the peanut crop, and this is a good section for it since it will be our cash crop; the rest being for stock feed.

I've been reading lots, of course, like the *Berlin Diary* (William Shirer) and *Flight to Arras* (Antoine de Saint-Exupéry). I've also been rereading Oswald Spengler's *Decline of the West*, and as something to settle my mind, George Santayana's philosophy.

I don't get very much writing done, and I've done a little knitting, only three pieces since the first of the year. I'm slow with it, not having as much time free, without interruption. Either there's sow farrowing, or calves breaking through the fence, or all the hens developing lice, or the dam breaking on the stock pond and Joe and I wading out at three in the morning to repair it with flashes of lightning all around us. Farm life isn't without its excitement. Ever play midwife to a sow?

Speaking of farrowing, I'm going to have a baby around the first of October. I can't tell you how sheepish I felt when I first discovered it, spacing my children fifteen years apart, and then I felt quite kittenish and young again. I tried to do this about three years ago, and had a pretty violent miscarriage, but since it's almost six months along now, I think everything will be lovely. We are all so happy about it. Ann's sage advice is awfully funny, part of her home economics last year was on pre-natal care, and to hear her bossing me around and taking care of me is most amusing. As for Joe, he thinks that at my age it might be a bit more difficult (37 doesn't seem too old to me). He galloped me in to our best OB man in Oklahoma City, and I'm really very satisfied with my doctor. He trained with Joseph Bolivar DeLee of Chicago and you know what miracles he performed in reforms for mothers. I feel anyone who worked with him is worth having.

A long paragraph, but this is quite an event for me after such a long time. I rather hope it will be twins. I feel more prepared now, for parenthood than when Ann was born. And I've had such a lot of pleasure and companionship and fun with her, that I'm looking forward to my new child. Who knows, I may have six more. What's Mrs. Dionne (mother of the Dionne Quintuplets, born May 28, 1934) got that I haven't, except quintuplets? And maybe if I squeezed, I could do as well.

Joe's mother wrote me desperately wanting me to go to her for the event but I'm staying here and go to the hospital when it's my time. As she said, she was afraid I'd have the baby midway between the pump and the chicken house and pick it up and put it under my arm and go on about my business. I can just see myself, years from now, telling little Joe Patrick, "Ah, well I do remember that frosty morning when you first saw the light of day in the pig pen!"

Well, this has been a long letter, and go thou and do likewise. I feel very proud of you for all your good works, and wish I could do as well, but mine's another obscurer sphere. Don't wear yourself out, however. All my love to both of you, and DO write soon.

Dollie

DOLLIE'S LAST LETTER, FUZZY AT BEST

May 3, 1947
Oklahoma City, Oklahoma

Dear Hazel:

I was very glad to get your letter when we came in this afternoon, and I decided I would answer at once, for it gives me the opportunity to talk to you, which I have not been able to avail myself of, because I lost your address, and your card at Christmas did not have the return address on it.

I was rather afraid at the time you must think me a complete nincompoop, and this has fretted me from time to time whenever I think of you. After I had finished talking with you on the phone, Joe asked me when I was belly aching at not having seen you, did you invite her to come up? And I did not remember whether or not I had, but I felt sure that you would know I wanted you to. It is a very bad habit of mine, assuming friends know I wish them to come by when they can, without waiting for my saying, "Well, come by and stay." Almost everyone we know does come without waiting when the opportunity presents itself. I suppose I forgot that there was the possibility that you might think me discourteous because of the lack of a formal invitation and I do beg your pardon, because it would have given me such a great pleasure for you to be here. I thought in my befuddled way, for even without the quantities of medicaments I was absorbing at the time, my mental processes are fuzzy at best, that you were too busy to come, that if you had been, you would without ado. So far this long period when we have had no communication, I have been stewing about it, and I am so glad of the chance to get it out of my system.

My house is dreadfully small, but we always manage to expand enough when friends come to see us. I found it very hard at the time you were here to go anywhere without my child. I have never liked to impose his care on my friends, since most of them have enough care of that sort of their own, and sitters were virtually non-existent at that time. This last year they have become more accessible and I do get a little time now and then. I think you have me confused. I do not have any friends who are nurses now and can't remember any then. You do know, however, I am sure how one's friends have a way of suddenly being gone from where you expect them to be, these later years. It's a restless world.

I am so glad you had a good time in the southwest. It is more than twenty-two years since I came here, and I have loved it from the start. I was intrigued, too, when I came, at the Main Line names in the country towns (Wynnewood – they say Winnie-wood here, Ardmore, Paoli, etc.). I too read the story in Holiday and prowled it out before. Oklahoma history is one of my things. I had the great privilege of having a friend of the late Robert S. Scivally of Ardmore. His daughter was and is still my friend. He, as one of the original founders of the town, filled me with its history, Bunyanesque and actual. They were the owners of the ranch now known as the Lazy S, which encompassed all of the Turner Falls country, and was then known as the Flying V.

The
Arbuckles
(the
Arbuckle
Mountains
are an
ancient
mountain range in south-central Oklahoma)
really are almost my hills of home, for I almost
forgotten the little, soft green hills of Ireland
(but never quite) and my courting was done in
and around the Arbuckles in one lovely April
and May. We drove through them this
afternoon and the slopes were flaming with
gaillardia and sheets of gold. Oh yes, we used to
drive that mountain road when it was a trifle
more perilous, with the moon making the hills
white, our bathing suits knotted on the door
handle and our hair still wet from swimming in
the Blue Hole below the falls. Now there are
cabins and people, there weren't then. And we

have fished Honey Creek and walked those hills so many times.

We drive down to Lake Murray almost every week, and now, we have our boats there. I do hope you see it, and Lake Texoma, when you come through, for they are both objects of great pride to Oklahomans, native and adopted. It's a long ride down and back, but worth it.

Joe had to give up his oil field job but his work with Wetherbee is very exacting, and the telephone is a little black devil from which there is no escape when we are in town. Yes, sanitary conditions in filling stations, etc. are in the main poor, though you find pleasant exceptions, but they prevail up through the northwest as we found on our Canadian fishing trips. But then, people with small children as a matter of course carry wash cloths and hand towels and tissues and creams. I have an over the shoulder bag I crocheted for myself that has developed into a sort of grandma's carry all, flashlights, camera, hair brushes, extra cigarettes, cosmetics, toothbrushes and cases, etc. I do agree that there is little more deplorable than the condition of "rest rooms."

It was a grand trip. I've was rather hampered by Ann first, and then Joe Pat, but I had a couple of years when I made a lot of trips with Joe to the fields in Illinois and Texas, and they were always fun. Driving together has always been something peculiarly intimate and stimulating. I am glad you liked the people you met in the Southwest, too. I think they are marvelous. I've always had such good friends and neighbors. So many of our friends from here have scattered during and after the war years, some not ever to return, others still friends by correspondence and occasional visits.

It was something nice, to have your picture chosen for the Eastman advertising. The next time you come perhaps you will have more time and can see some of the wild and lovely country in southeastern Oklahoma. The Kismichi Mountains are subjects for photography in almost any season. There is now an annual dogwood pilgrimage to that section since the country is unbelievably beautiful. You'd love the names there, the Winding Stair Mountain Range, Luksicolo (many turtles) Creek (years ago we'd go there to fish, catch so many you couldn't get them in the car), Eagletown, Broken Bow, Antlers and the Ozark trip is one to make, too. That's lovely country and used to be marvelous fishing. We haven't been up for years, so I don't know about now.

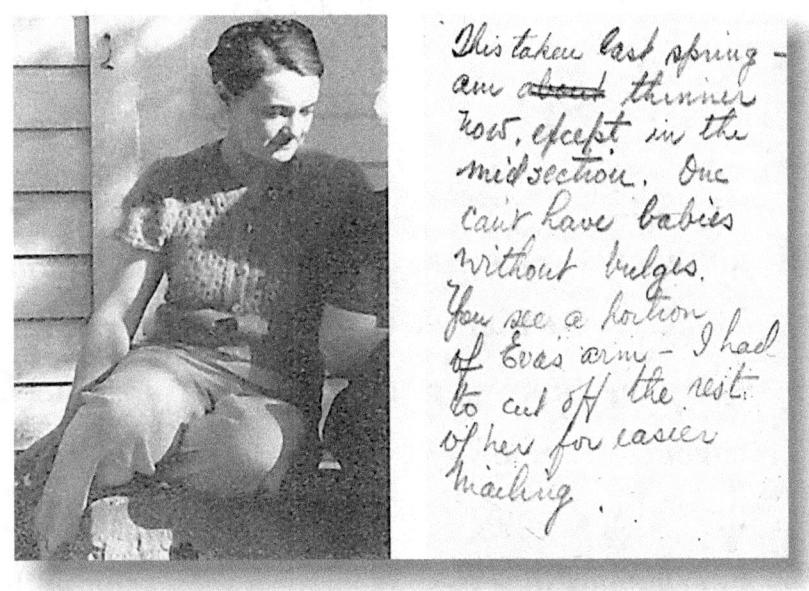

(Dollie's photo and note on the reverse)

I was happy that at least you saw my
Ann. With the unreasonable prejudice of a
mother, I am very fond of her. She is working
very hard, and for such a youngster, doing very
well. I was disappointed that she went to work
without any college training, but if she doesn't
marry in a year or so, I think she is going to
take time off to enter medical school. I can't see
that she is like me at all, though so many people

think so, but her features seem very dissimilar to mine.

Yes, I expect my voice has changed after all these years, yours too was not quite the same to me. At the time we talked, however, I was doing one of my periodic bronchial flips, I have chronic bronchitis, so I might have sounded a little deeper than usual. We all recovered from our various illnesses. We are so very seldom ill, that it was really unusual. But when we do get ill, we do it all at once and as horribly as possible. I have had a beastly time this spring with all of us having "flu." Joe really very ill and Ann prostrated (she's a fragile looking little thing, but she has the constitution of a Shetland pony) and Joe Pattie having two relapses. I think now the wet spring seems broken and that good, hot sun is out again and we will all be better. I am just in from yesterday afternoon and I am a cat for sunshine and today I got my first burn, and I feel grand.

You spoke of a recent picture of me, and I have only some snapshots taken last summer. I have reached the age when the fewer pictures taken of me, the better. The only trouble is that our friend Pat is an avid picture taker, and when he does take one of me, it is when I am least expecting it and so I never have time to rearrange "that sorry scheme of things," that

happens to be my face. I still have no grey hair, but many wrinkles and find myself preferring the non-violent pleasures. I am enclosing some snapshots (I always have plenty, so don't bother to return them as before. Ann messes with pictures quite a lot (develops, etc.). There's one of Joe, one with Joe Patrick and me and our boat, the Anni

(the Turtle V is visible behind us). It is the boat Joe and his brother-in-law Gordon made, but we have added another, the Turtle VI, which is our darling just now; a sixteen-footer with a fifty horsepower outboard. It fairly skims. We are boat poor.

Looking at these pictures I must say I am doing my hair a different way, but it is the same old chassis. It was brought home to me how people change recently when the girl who preceded me in Joe's affections, and whom we have not seen in twenty years, wired us that she was coming through and came out at two in the morning and stayed until ten in the morning. When we knew her she was small and smart, and oh, soigneée. Now, well, it is apparent that the years have gone over. So I cannot feel that I am unaltered. In fact, I know damn well I'm not.

This is a really very long letter, and it is late and I must rise early, so shall cease here. I do hope that neither sickness nor misunderstanding interferes with our meeting the next time. It is possible I may go north again to see my mother soon and, if I do, I will certainly try to see you.

Love,
Dollie

THE LETTERS END

The May 3, 1947 letter was her last and there was no more information about Dollie in Hazel's collection.

Records indicate that Joe William McFarlane died in Alameda, California in 1967 when he was 62. Dollie passed away three years later in Santa Clara, California. She was 65.

I'm conjecturing that perhaps they or their children moved to the west coast and they followed. There's no way to know for sure.

Hazel died of cancer in New Jersey in 1981 when she was 77. She had been married to Mac for 53 years. They did not have children.

After marrying Marie Collins in 1981, Harold "Mac" McClary died in New Jersey in

1989. He was 87 years old. Oddly enough,
Mac's mother's name was Maude, the same as
Dollie's middle name.

Harold "Mac"
McClary, during
WW II

SELECTED SAMPLES OF DOLLIE'S WRITINGS

(June 5, 1923) Sunset - a molten lake of gold in the West, the eastern clouds flushed a delicate rose, against a pastel blue sky. Below, trees a feathery mass of contrasting greens and brown, and the scent of purified fields of alfalfa, sweet in my nostrils.

(June 21, 1923) I want you to know, as you surely must, that I have always felt towards you a tenderness that I have felt for no other being. A vague wanting to shield, to help, to love - oh, it's indefinable, but, you understand.

(June 11, 1923) All afternoon I wiped the
perspiration from various portions of my
anatomy and have watched the heat simmer in
waves out of the ground. Watched sombreroed
tanned men drive horses, white with lather,
across sandy hollows. To turn and typewrite
madly, wipe away more sweat, turn and watch
tractors crawl through the blazing sunshine.
There a line of trees, greener than grass, against
the blue, burning skyline. A mule team passes,
the mules back their heads to bray with disgust
at the intensity of the heat. It's frightful – I've
never experienced anything like it – I'm
radiating heat like one of those beastly old-
fashioned German porcelain stoves.

(June 21, 1923) Child, never, never be afraid of losing my esteem and love, my emotional outbursts. Why, they're part of you, dear - they're scraps of my Hazel that I treasure more than untold gold. If you must leash yourself before others who cannot understand, to me tell everything. I know the feeling, I understand, and love.

Last night I prayed that I might be worthy of your love, and always keep it for life would be empty and hollow without it. And, I cried, Hazel, cried tears of impotence and longing, helplessness and yearning. I wanted so to be with you, to try humbly to make up the love you need.

(May 31, 1926) Perhaps I was abrupt, but so was my marriage. You see, I only knew Joe for six weeks and then we came to the conclusion that there was no use in being so uselessly and needlessly separated. And so we were married, very quietly and circumspectly, with two of Joe's friends as our witnesses, at their house.

(May 31, 1926) But, oh, it's hard to be sane. We live in an impossibly idyllic little white house, with a picket fence, and great crimson roses dripping from the trellises. And at night a great musical comedy, golden moon tears itself from the arms of the silent trees to shine for us, as we sit on the porch, Joe at my feet, his dear dark head against my knee, and our cigarettes glowing, turn circles of fire. And I had not known that life could be so very dear. I love. I am loved. We're young. The gods are kind. Too kind. Sometimes I fear that they may become jealous of my happiness.

(June 19, 1942) I've been, for four or five years, a Cassandra crying woe! Woe! Upon the steps of the temple, but being justified in having said so doesn't make me happier. I hate the whole beastly business of war, so who doesn't? I wish there were some way that I could do more; to help and serve.

(May 3, 1947) I think now the wet spring seems broken and that good, hot sun is out again and we will all be better. I am just in from yesterday afternoon and I am a cat for sunshine and today I got my first burn, and I feel grand.

(May 3, 1947) The Arbuckles (The Arbuckle
Mountains are an ancient mountain range in
south-central Oklahoma) really are almost my
hills of home, for I almost forgotten the little,
soft green hills of Ireland (but never quite) and
my courting was done in and around the
Arbuckles in one lovely April and May. We
drove through them this afternoon and the
slopes were flaming with gaillardia and sheets
of gold. Oh yes, we used to drive that mountain
road when it was a trifle more perilous, with the
moon making the hills white, our bathing suits
knotted on the door handle and our hair still
wet from swimming in the Blue Hole below the
falls. Now there are cabins and people, there
weren't then. And we have fished Honey Creek
and walked those wills so many times.

FINAL COMMENT
By T. J. Hickey

Picture Dollie and her family facing poverty and repression, escaping the "Easter Uprising" against the English in 1916, and leaving their beloved Ireland for a life full of uncertainty in America.

Quietly emerging from this narrative is a heartwarming story of a strong and passionate young woman willing to tackle unknown adventures – along with their inherent dangers – far from home.

Dollie was smart and self-reliant, as evidenced by her pilfering a neighbor's provisions in support of her family, and then thoroughly enjoying the adventure. This portrayal alone provides readers with a glimpse into the heart and mind of a bold, strong and creative Dollie, someone with an astonishing will to prevail despite numerous obstacles, ones to which a lesser person would succumb.

Letters from Dollie reveals a woman with an active imagination, whose family avoided the squalor of the big cities, where many Irish before had settled, choosing instead remote places in Kansas and Oklahoma that reminded her of her native land.

While we only get snapshots of Dollie's life through her letters, we can't help but appreciate the fortitude of this amazing woman!

T. J. Hickey is the author of *A Soldier's Story* and *Surviving The Great Depression*.

ABOUT THE AUTHOR

Joaquin Bowman is a retired transportation executive and teacher. He has published three books in his memoir series: *Tadville, Suscipiat Dominus* and, most recently, *The Sam and Don Show – Lost Episodes.* In addition he prepared two biographies for the Library of Congress' Veterans History Project: *Tom Hickey's India – 1945-1946, and Bill Topkis – Liberation of Nordhausen.* In 2014 he co-produced Tom Hickey's *Surviving the Great Depression* and co-authored *Words and Works* with his wife Mary Ann. Mr. Bowman enjoys photography and has exhibited at several Bucks County shows. He is

 a member of the Broadcast Pioneers of Philadelphia and the Sons of the American Revolution.

The couple has four children and nine grandchildren. They live in Bucks County, Pennsylvania.